CHRIS BUSH

Chris Bush is an award-w
maker and an Associate D_____ __ _____ _____ ___ __ ____
includes *Rock / Paper / Scissors* (Sheffield Theatres), *Jane Eyre*
(Stephen Joseph Theatre/New Vic Theatre), *Fantastically Great
Women Who Changed the World* (Kenny Wax, UK tour), *Hungry*
(Paines Plough), *Kein Weltuntergang / (Not) The End of the World*
(Schaubühne, Berlin), *Standing at the Sky's Edge* (Sheffield
Theatres – Best Theatre: South Bank Sky Arts Awards; Best
Musical: UK Theatre Awards), *Nine Lessons and Carols: Stories
for a Long Winter* (Almeida Theatre), *Faustus: That Damned
Woman* (Headlong/Lyric Hammersmith/Birmingham Rep), *The
Last Noël* (Attic Theatre/UK tour), *The Assassination of Katie
Hopkins* (Theatr Clwyd – Best Musical: UK Theatre Awards),
Pericles (National Theatre: Olivier), *The Changing Room* (NT
Connections), *The Band Plays On, Steel, What We Wished For,
A Dream, The Sheffield Mysteries* (all Sheffield Theatres), *Scenes
from the End of the World* (Yard/Central School), *A Declaration
from the People* (National Theatre: Dorfman) and *Larksong* (New
Vic, Stoke-on-Trent). Awards include a South Bank Sky Arts
Award, two UK Theatre Awards, the Perfect Pitch Award, a Brit
Writers' Award and the Theatre Royal Haymarket Writers' Award.

RICHARD HAWLEY

Richard Hawley is synonymous with his native city of Sheffield. He has released nine studio albums over the last twenty years, with two being nominated for the Mercury Music Prize. He is also a Brit nominee and received a South Bank Award in 2007.

Over the years, Richard has become as well known for his guitar-playing as his singing. He has duetted with Tom Jones, Nancy Sinatra and Shirley Bassey, and played with Arctic Monkeys, Elbow, Paul Weller, Manic Street Preachers and Pulp, the band he played guitar with for a number of years.

Best known for his mix of classic songwriting, soothing vocals and northern grit realism, Richard is something of a unique artist in British popular music, being able to cross boundaries from one musical style to another whilst keeping intact his own strong identity.

STANDING AT THE SKY'S EDGE

Book by
Chris Bush

Music & Lyrics by
Richard Hawley

NICK HERN BOOKS

London
www.nickhernbooks.co.uk

A Nick Hern Book

Standing at the Sky's Edge first published in Great Britain as a paperback original in 2022 by Nick Hern Books Limited, The Glasshouse, 49a Goldhawk Road, London W12 8QP

Cover photograph (of Rachael Wooding, Faith Omole and Bobbie Little) by Sam Wright

Designed and typeset by Nick Hern Books, London
Printed in Great Britain by Mimeo Ltd, Huntingdon, Cambridgeshire
PE29 6XX

A CIP catalogue record for this book is available from the British Library

ISBN 978 1 83904 147 1

Woodland
CARBON
www.woodlandcarbon.co.uk
NICK HERN BOOKS
Printed on Carbon Captured paper

For everyone who's made a home here

Introduction
Chris Bush

It's now been almost ten years since I wrote my first play for Sheffield Theatres, and I believe my tally now stands in the double digits. Almost every one of those pieces has been described by someone at some point as a 'love letter' to Sheffield. More often than not, I haven't been aware that's what I was writing. In fact, while this label has generally been used approvingly, sometimes it's irked me a little. As a writer I want to be in the business of nuance and complexity, not hagiography. Aren't love letters a bit simplistic? Don't they sit at odds with the knotty and three-dimensional portraits I'm trying to create?

Recently I've come to accept the compliment. After all, love is knotty. Love is three-dimensional. To love something is not to declare it flawless, but to love it in spite of, or even because of, its flaws. Love can sometimes be difficult to explain, impossible to justify rationally, but this only makes it more interesting. Beauty, as we know, is in the eye of the beholder, and this is because love is really just a matter of perspective – it's the lens through which we observe the object of our affection. The same faces, the same streets, the same rolling hills or rain-streaked concrete, these things become loveable when looked on lovingly. If I have spent the last decade writing inadvertent love letters to this remarkable city, perhaps it's only because I can't see it any other way. Love is in the looking.

Park Hill has not always been an easy place to love. Built with all the best intentions, it wasn't long before problems started to arise. In fact, one former resident told me that the roof was leaking within the first year of it being open. For some, it's an architectural icon. For others, it's always been an eyesore. Whatever its aesthetic merits or lofty ideals, it's undeniable that for a significant part of its history it did a fairly terrible job of fulfilling the function it was built for. Shelter is not just about keeping out the rain (and, as noted, it didn't always do that very well), but it's about security, community, comfort, a sense of belonging, a source of pride. At its lowest ebb, the only residents of Park Hill were those who had no means to be anywhere else. As such, it did shelter some of the city's most vulnerable, but not with the dignity or care to which we're all entitled. And yet, as Connie tells us:

> *Love blossoms in the most unlikely places*
> *Love amongst the piss-smelling walkways*
> *The world's most effective air freshener*

Not love for the building, perhaps love *in spite of* the building, but still love to find here nonetheless. Love, and endurance, and a belief that things can get better. These characters aren't idiots, they're not hopelessly naive or absurdly optimistic, in fact they might often struggle to make it to the end of each day, but they are trying to make a home here, to put down roots, to make the most of the hand they've been dealt.

From one perspective, *Standing at the Sky's Edge* is a hyper-local story – the action is mostly contained within one flat on one estate in one city – but beyond that, it is the story of post-war Britain in microcosm. While this wasn't always at the forefront of my mind while writing, Park Hill has increasingly come to embody the state itself – designed as a force for good by people who perhaps never fully understood who they were building it for, underfunded, monolithic and unwieldy, a money pit, a monumental feat, an idealistic and unsustainable albatross. As national fortunes change so does its function, shifting from something designed for everyone to a not-fit-for-purpose last resort, avoided by all but the most at risk. Then, as we approach the modern era, its nature changes again – it is revitalised, it dazzles, the concrete gleams, but this is only possible through private investment, and now it serves a different type of person, its function has shifted once more, it's no longer the thing it was built for.

Of course this is an oversimplification, and by no means an exact parallel. Park Hill remains a complicated proposition with a chequered history, which is one of the reasons why its story is worth telling. It *is* beautiful now. The new flats – all sympathetically and lavishly refurbished – are a patchwork of private, social and student housing. It has avoided demolition and rebuilt itself for a new century. From an outside view, it appears to be working. Whatever mistakes were made, whatever it could've done better, it is at least serving a function again – it is a home – it is *hundreds* of homes, each one of them containing a story. It will house locals, and those who will become local, given time. It will provide shelter, and hopefully a great deal more than that. It is not without its flaws. It cannot be all things to all people, and perhaps has strayed far too far from its initial brief. Not everyone is able to look upon it lovingly, and I understand that. And so I don't think this is a love letter to Park Hill itself, not to the steel and the concrete, not to the monolith, but most certainly to the people within it, to all of them, to the ones who thrived and the ones who struggled, the ones who got out and the ones who clung on. To the ones who made a home here.

While we're on the subject of love – this show would be nothing without the sheer brilliance of Richard Hawley, and the aching, deeply felt romance that carries through all his work, masterfully orchestrated by Tom Deering. Much love too for Ben Stones and his stunning design, finding the beauty in the Brutalism, for Lynne Page's gorgeous movement, and Rupert Lord's sheer bloody-mindedness in getting us all this far. I love that the National Theatre have recognised this is a properly national story, and invited us to play with them. I love this phenomenal company of actors, filled with old friends and new discoveries, and I must, as always, save the largest part of my (professional) love for Rob Hastie, not only the finest director, but the nicest man in British Theatre. I am beyond privileged to be able to work with such an amazing team, and to get to tell these stories all over again.

December 2022

Standing at the Sky's Edge was co-commissioned by Sheffield Theatres and Various Productions Ltd. It was first performed at the Crucible Theatre, Sheffield, on 20 March 2019 (previews from 14 March). It was revived at the Crucible on 15 December 2022 (previews from 10 December), then transferred to the Olivier auditorium at the National Theatre, London, on 13 February 2023 (previews from 9 February).

The cast for this revival production was as follows:

WORKMAN 1/GARY/NIGEL	Darragh Cowley
WORKMAN 3/KEVIN/MAX/ DANCE CAPTAIN	Ahmed Hamad
JUSTINE	Séverine Howell-Meri
JIMMY	Samuel Jordan
CONNIE	Bobbie Little
HARRY	Robert Lonsdale
WORKMAN 2	David McKechnie
NIKKI	Maimuna Memon
CATHY	Rachael Louise Miller
GEORGE	Baker Mukasa
MARCUS/HOUSING OFFICER	Alastair Natkiel
JOY	Faith Omole
CHARLES/TREV/SEB	Adam Price
JENNY	Consuela Rolle
VIVIENNE/KAREN	Nicola Sloane
TEEN	Jake Small
GRACE/ALICE	Deborah Tracey
ROSE	Rachael Wooding
POPPY	Alex Young
YOUNG CONNIE	Amira Anderson, Hallie Barthram, Neriah Boakye
YOUNG JIMMY	William Barker, Luke Beggs, Harry Weston

The cast in Sheffield were supported by a community chorus from Sheffield People's Theatre, and in London by a supernumerary chorus.

UNDERSTUDIES
JIMMY/TEEN   Darragh Cowley
CONNIE/NIKKI   Sèverine Howell-Meri
CHARLES/TREV/SEB/   David McKechnie
    MARCUS
ROSE/POPPY/VIVIENNE   Rachael Louise Miller
GEORGE   Ahmed Hamad
HARRY   Alastair Natkiel
JOY/GRACE   Consuela Rolle
KEVIN/HOUSING OFFICER/   Jake Small
    WORKMAN 1, 2 & 3/GARY/
    NIGEL/MAX

Music Director / Keys 1   John Rutledge
Assistant Music Director /   Ehsaan Shivarani
    Keys 2 / Guitar
Lead Guitars   Neil Brock
Electric & Upright Bass   Phil Donnelly
Drum Kit & Percussion   Darren Beckett
Violin   Andra Vonricu
Violin 2 / Viola   Sally Belcher
                                   and Una Palliser
Cello   Gabriella Swallow
                                   and Verity Simmons

Director   Robert Hastie
Set and Costume Designer   Ben Stones
Choreographer   Lynne Page
Music Supervisor, Arranger   Tom Deering
    and Orchestrator
Lighting Designer   Mark Henderson
Sound Designer   Bobby Aitken
Wigs, Hair and Make-up Designer Cynthia De La Rosa
Music Director   John Rutledge
Casting Director   Stuart Burt CDG
Additional Casting   Chloe Blake
Staff Director   Elin Schofield
Associate Choreographer   Thomas Herron
    and Staff Director (London run)
Associate Costume Designer   Sally Wilson

Fight Director	Kenan Ali
Dialect Coach	Michaela Kennen
Dialect Coach	Shereen Ibrahim
Assistant Musical Director	Ehsaan Shivarani
Rehearsal Pianist	Tom Crathorne
Music Preparation	Matthew Jackson
Producers	John Tomlinson (ST), Rachel Quinney (NT), Rupert Lord (VP)
Assistant Producers	James Ashfield (ST), Larah Simpson (VP)
Trainee Producer	Miranda Debenham (ST)
Production Manager	Anthony Newton
Stage Manager	Sarah Gentle
Deputy Stage Manager	Sarah Greenwood
Assistant Stage Manager	Edie Fitt-Martin
Rehearsal Assistant Stage Manager	Kimberley Towler

Characters

The piece moves between three different timelines, as follows:

TIMELINE A: 1960/1979/1985/1989
TIMELINE B: 1989/1992/2002/2004
TIMELINE C: 2015/2017/2019/2020

TIMELINE A:
ROSE, *local. Slightly unwilling housewife. Begins mid-twenties*
HARRY, *her husband. Steel worker. Begins mid-twenties*
JAMES, *their son, age eight*
TREV, *a former colleague of Harry*
NIGEL, *Trev's son*
CATHY, *Nigel's fiancée*

TIMELINE B:
JOY, *a young Liberian refugee. Begins age fourteen*
GRACE, *her elder cousin*
GEORGE, *another of Joy's cousins, Grace's younger brother*
JIMMY, *the now-teenage son of Harry and Rose*
CONSTANCE, *Joy's daughter. Begins ten*
HOUSING OFFICER
GARY, *a local teen*
KEVIN, *a local teen*
TEEN

TIMELINE C:
POPPY, *southern, middle class. Thirties*
NIKKI, *Poppy's ex. Twenties/thirties*
CHARLES, *Poppy's father. Fifties/sixties*
VIVIENNE, *Poppy's mother. Fifties/sixties*
MARCUS, *Poppy's colleague. Thirties*
CONNIE, *adult Constance, now mid-twenties*
MAX, *Marcus's boyfriend*
SEB, *party guest*
ALICE, *party guest*

KAREN, *party guest*
JUSTINE, *party guest*
JENNY, *party guest*

Additionally WORKMEN (1–3) *and* COMPANY *play various other choral roles as indicated.*

Note

No real attempt has been made to denote accents/spell dialogue phonetically (other than in a few specific instances), as by and large this is patronising and unhelpful, but allow the Sheffield dialect to inform all local characters.

This text went to press before the end of rehearsals and so may differ slightly from the play as performed.

Musical Numbers

ACT ONE

'As the Dawn Breaks'	WORKMAN 1/ ROSE/JOY/ POPPY
'Time Is'	COMPANY
'Naked in Pitsmoor'	POPPY
'I'm Looking for Someone to Find Me'	ROSE/POPPY/ COMPANY
'Tonight the Streets Are Ours'	GEORGE/ COMPANY

ACT TWO

'Open Up Your Door'	NIKKI
'My Little Treasures'	HARRY/ COMPANY
'Coles Corner'	JOY
'There's a Storm A-Comin''	COMPANY

ACT THREE

'Standing at the Sky's Edge'   COMPANY

'Our Darkness'   NIGEL/CATHY/
                                            HARRY/ROSE/
                                            COMPANY

'Midnight Train'   JIMMY/
                                            COMPANY

'For Your Lover Give Some Time'   HARRY/POPPY/
                                            NIKKI

'There's a Storm A-Comin'' (Reprise)   JOY

ACT FOUR

'After the Rain'   ROSE/COMPANY

'Don't Get Hung Up in Your Soul'   CONNIE/JIMMY/
                                            JOY

'As the Dawn Breaks' (Reprise)   ROSE/JOY/
                                            POPPY/NIKKI
                                            COMPANY

ACT ONE

Scene One

*Park Hill flats. Early morning – bright, cold. A neon sign
reading 'I love you will u marry me?' is suspended above the
stage. A young* WORKMAN *in a high-vis jacket enters with
a Thermos of tea. He stops to look out over the city.*

Song: 'As the Dawn Breaks'

WORKMAN 1. AS THE DAWN BREAKS
  OVER ROOF SLATES
  HOPE HUNG ON EVERY WASHING LINE

  AS YOUR HEART ACHES
  OVER LIFE'S FATE
  I KNOW WE NEVER HAD MUCH TIME

  FOR US TO GIVE
  BUT WE DID
  THERE'S SOMETHING IN THOSE DEEP BLUE EYES

  AS THE LIGHT CREEPS OVER THE HOUSES
  AND THE SLATES ARE DARKED BY RAIN
  IN THIS MORNING SEARCH FOR MEANING
  I HEAR A SONGBIRD'S MELODY

  I HEAR A SONGBIRD'S MELODY
  AND SHE'S SINGING JUST FOR ME

Two more WORKMEN *enter. Toolkits, fuse readers, etc.*

WORKMAN 2. You helping, or what?

WORKMAN 1. Yeah, coming. (*Still looking out.*) Not bad
  though, is it?

WORKMAN 3 (*head buried in a mobile phone*). What?

  Sighs from the other two.

  (*More indignant.*) What?

WORKMAN 1. Look – don't you ever just look at it?

WORKMAN 3. Why? Not going anywhere, is it?

WORKMAN 2. Alright then, let's get to it – see what's gone wrong this time.

WORKMAN 1. Always summat.

WORKMAN 3. That neon's been a bastard since day one.

WORKMAN 1. Should've left it as graffiti.

WORKMAN 3. Should've torn the whole place down when they had the chance.

WORKMAN 2. Nah. Life in it yet.

Our focus shifts to three different tenants arriving at Park Hill in three separate years. They each hold a bag or a box. Whenever we move years we somehow see the date displayed clearly on the set.

First to enter is ROSE *in 1960. She takes in the view, a little awestruck.*

ROSE. AS THE LIGHT CREEPS OVER THE HOUSES
AND THE SLATES ARE DARKED BY RAIN

Now in 2015, POPPY *arrives outside her flat. Hopeful.*

POPPY. IN THIS MORNING SEARCH FOR MEANING
I HEAR A SONGBIRD'S MELODY

Finally, JOY *arrives in 1989. She is mostly terrified, trying to be brave.*

JOY. I HEAR A SONGBIRD'S MELODY
AND SHE'S SINGING JUST FOR ME

The three women sing in harmony, looking out.

ROSE/JOY/POPPY. OH SHE'S SINGING JUST FOR ME
A SIMPLE SONGBIRD'S MELODY

The neon sign flickers on.

WORKMAN 2. Right. That'll hold it for now, come on.

The WORKMEN *go.* CONNIE, *an estate agent, emerges.*
She's smartly dressed and holds a clipboard. She addresses
the audience. As CONNIE *talks,* ROSE, JOY *and* POPPY
have a moment, taking in the flat. Music underneath.

CONNIE. Three mornings, decades apart
Same old sun
That makes optimists of the lovesick
Restarts the hearts of old romantics
And roly-polies irrepressibly down the hillside
Hitting the concrete
With the full force of a first kiss.

Three households, decades apart
Sharing one roof, one sun, one hope
To root themselves
Become an eighth hill
In this man-made monolith
To matter to someone
To make something of their days
As the dawn breaks
And breaths are held
Because this moment won't come again.
Savour the stillness, then –

She goes. Straight into –

Scene Two

Music kicks up a notch – propulsive, uplifting. JOY *and* POPPY
go, and we arrive in 1960, where HARRY *joins* ROSE *outside*
their flat. He's carrying a heavy box. A FIGURE *appears above*
them with a microphone and sings.

Song: 'Time Is'

FIGURE. WHERE HAVE WE BEEN TO
AND WHAT DID YOU SEE?

DON'T REALLY KNOW WHY
BUT IT DOESN'T BOTHER ME

TIME IS ON YOUR SIDE RIGHT NOW
BUT TIME CAN CHANGE

HARRY. Hold up!

HARRY pants. ROSE chuckles.

ROSE. Sorry!

HARRY (*putting the box down*). Spare a thought for your pack mule.

ROSE. I couldn't wait. Just look at it.

HARRY. Just let me catch me breath. Then I'll go back for the next one.

ROSE. Can you imagine watching the sunrise from up here?

HARRY. I'd sooner have a lie-in.

ROSE. You, Harry Stanhope, have no sense of romance.

HARRY. Is that right, Mrs Stanhope?

They kiss.

ROSE. Do you want to see inside?

HARRY. Still got boxes on the street.

ROSE. Come on –

HARRY. And Trev's sat waiting with the van.

ROSE. Just a peek.

HARRY. We should get these stacked, finish off downstairs, make sure… (*Off her look.*) Alright! Let's be having you then.

ROSE. I beg your pardon?

HARRY. If we're doing this, we're doing it properly.

He picks up ROSE. She protests, but is delighted.

ROSE (*laughing*). What are you doing? Put me down – you'll put your back out!

HARRY. I'm just a born romantic.

He grunts a little as he carries her across the threshold and offstage. Song continues.

FIGURE. WHAT IS IT THAT YOU'RE WANTING
AND WHAT ARE YOU HIDING?
DO YOU KNOW WHERE IT IS YOU'RE GOING TO
AND HOPING TO FIND THERE?

COMPANY. TIME IS ON YOUR SIDE RIGHT NOW
BUT TIME WILL CHANGE

We now jump to 1989. JOY returns with her older cousins GRACE and GEORGE, being shown round the flat by a housing OFFICER. They also have their possessions with them, a few odds and ends gathered in backpacks and carrier bags. They appear shell-shocked.

OFFICER (*speaking slowly and clearly*). Here's your kitchen. Kitchen, yeah? Sink, for water? Water comes out here.

GRACE. Yes.

OFFICER. For washing up, and for drinking. You can drink it.

The OFFICER mimes drinking. GRACE nods.

Oven, here. Hot. Um. This hob isn't working… Fridge – quite new – not bad. Fridge is for… You know what a fridge is for.

GRACE. Yes.

OFFICER. Great. And the door – your front door – you always lock it, yeah? Locked and bolted. You wouldn't want… This door. Locked. Keep out bad men. (*Beat.*) Right. Good luck. I'll leave you to it.

He goes.

JOY (*to GRACE*). Why was he speaking like that? Do you think there was something wrong with him?

GRACE. Come on – let's put these things away.

They go.

FIGURE. AS YOU ARE NOW
I ONCE WAS
AS I AM NOW
YOU WILL BE

COMPANY. TIME IS ON YOUR SIDE RIGHT NOW
BUT TIME WILL CHANGE

We jump again to 2015. POPPY, early thirties, middle class, southern, is being let into her new home by CONNIE. This is one of the newly refurbished apartments. Sparse but undeniably stylish.

CONNIE. That's you all set then. Any questions, you know where I am.

POPPY. Thanks.

CONNIE. Happy?

POPPY. It's beautiful, isn't it?

CONNIE. I think so. Bit different from when I grew up round here –

POPPY. I can imagine.

CONNIE. But that's no bad thing. New lick of paint, new lease of life. Right time for a new set of people.

CONNIE *gives* POPPY *her keys.*

POPPY. Yeah. I think it's going to be great here – really great.

CONNIE *goes.* POPPY *takes in the space.*

FIGURE. TO MY STONE-BRED SONS
AND MY HURRICANE DAUGHTER
WE WERE BORN FROM SAND
AND TO SAND WE WILL RETURN
AND WIND AND WHITE WATER

COMPANY. TIME IS ON YOUR SIDE RIGHT NOW
   TIME WILL CHANGE
   TIME WILL CHANGE
   TIME WILL CHANGE

Song ends.

Scene Three

A shift. We settle in 2015. VIVIENNE *and* CHARLES, *Poppy's
parents, enter.* VIVIENNE *holds a tray of tea.*

VIVIENNE. I found teabags, but I couldn't see milk.

POPPY. Sorry, I haven't had the chance yet.

CHARLES. Do you want us to nip out?

POPPY. Can you live without? I've got Ocado coming later –
   all the basics.

CHARLES. We'll survive.

VIVIENNE. Can you get Ocado up here?

POPPY. It's South Yorkshire, Mum, not Siberia.

CHARLES. It's magnificent. The finish is just… I have to say,
   lollipop, I think you've done very well.

VIVIENNE. I'm sure once you've warmed it up a little –

CHARLES. It's Brutalism, it isn't meant to be warm! (*To*
   POPPY.) Don't listen to the heathen. No. Extraordinary –
   historic – you're living in one of the largest listed buildings
   in Europe, did you know that?

VIVIENNE. They'll be sticking a blue plaque on Spaghetti
   Junction next.

CHARLES. Streets in the Sky – Le Corbusier –

VIVIENNE. But is it… Do you suppose it's *safe* here?

POPPY. Compared to where I was?

CHARLES. Yes, I think Basra is still safer than Brixton. Although they do get a bit radical this far north – you'll have to check for Reds under the bed.

POPPY *rolls her eyes*.

VIVIENNE. I just worry about all the others boarded up, standing empty.

POPPY. They won't be for long. They're going to redevelop the whole estate.

VIVIENNE. You're moving into a building site then?

POPPY (*ignoring this*). And the demand was crazy. There was a waiting list – people queueing down the street.

CHARLES. I'm not surprised. Honestly, I'm amazed you can afford all this.

POPPY. So was I. And that view! I'm in love with it.

VIVIENNE. I suppose as flats go…

POPPY. It's a split-level duplex.

VIVIENNE. It's just a big change – a sudden –

POPPY (*firmly*). Change is good.

VIVIENNE. And you were doing so well – you seemed to be doing so well in London, really getting somewhere, and to just run away from all that –

POPPY. I'm not running away –

VIVIENNE. I didn't –

POPPY. I'm starting over.

VIVIENNE. All I meant was –

POPPY. I'll be managing my own team, I'm on the property ladder, I –

VIVIENNE. I know.

POPPY. You know the woman, the estate agent who showed me round, she actually grew up here, before they did all this. She talked about family, *community*.

CHARLES. And you haven't spoken to Nikki at all?

POPPY. I can't. You know I can't.

CHARLES. Only the way things ended between you –

POPPY. It's not about that. That's not why… It was toxic – that whole city is toxic, and… It isn't running away. It isn't. I don't know why you'd say that.

VIVIENNE. Alright! It's fabulous. Very chic. Just a long way from home, that's all.

POPPY (*as an olive branch*). Only two hours to St Pancras. And look – you can see the station from here.

VIVIENNE. Yes. (*Beat.*) I'm sure you'll be very happy here.

CHARLES. We should probably… We should get on the motorway before rush hour – if there's nothing else you need us for.

POPPY. Yeah, sure. (*Gesturing to boxes.*) And I should get on with all of this.

CHARLES. Love you, lollipop.

VIVIENNE. We're only a phone call away.

POPPY. Thanks. Thank you. Sorry. And text me when you're home, please.

They hug goodbye and CHARLES *and* VIVIENNE *go.*
POPPY *sighs and collects herself.*

Scene Four

POPPY *stays onstage, moving aside, perhaps starting to unpack. Elsewhere, back in 1989,* JOY *enters with a tatty bag of possessions. She opens it up, looking for something, eventually finding an old, battered music box. She lies on her stomach and winds the box up, letting it play. Music plays, which will form the opening bars of 'Naked in Pitsmoor'.*

Song: 'Naked in Pitsmoor'

POPPY. I LEFT MY LIFE SOMEWHERE BEHIND
    MY SCREWED-UP EYES DON'T SEEM TO SHINE
    SINCE THE DAY YOU SAID GOODBYE
    I JUST DON'T SEEM TO TRY, IT'S TRUE
    OH IT'S SO TRUE

    GEORGE *comes out to join* JOY.

GEORGE. It's still working?

JOY. Yes.

GEORGE. A miracle.

JOY. Yes.

GEORGE. A good sign.

    JOY *closes the music box. The music stops.*

JOY. We're not going home, are we?

GEORGE. You should think of this as home for now.

JOY. I thought you said this was just a holiday.

GEORGE. You see your room, eh? You see the view?

JOY. Where do you think my parents are now?

GEORGE. Guinea. They will be safe in Guinea.

JOY. And when will they come here?

GEORGE. You should unpack your things – it's been long enough.

JOY. I don't want to. I don't want to stay here.

GEORGE. I know – but we have no choice for now.

JOY. But why?

GEORGE. Joy –

JOY. What do you know?

GEORGE. I've told you –

JOY. Tell me the truth!

GEORGE. What truth? What do you think I know? Truth is you should be grateful. Truth is you are only our cousin – we didn't have to take you. Truth is if we had left you where you were… (*He can't finish the thought.*)

JOY. Then what? Say it.

GEORGE. Unpack your shit. I'm sick of your bags lying around. We're not going anywhere.

He turns and starts to go.

JOY. George?

He stops.

You think they made it to Guinea? You think that's where they are now?

GEORGE. I do, yes.

GEORGE *goes.* JOY *exits.* POPPY *picks up the song.*

POPPY. I LEFT MY LIFE SOMEWHERE BEHIND
MY SCREWED-UP EYES DON'T SEEM TO SHINE
SINCE THE DAY YOU SAID GOODBYE
I JUST DON'T SEEM TO TRY, IT'S TRUE
OH IT'S SO TRUE

WHAT HAVE YOU DONE TO ME, BABY?
I'M JUST WASTED
AND WAKE IN THE MORNING
AND GET UP SCREAMING

YOU GAVE YOUR LIGHT TO SOMEONE NEW
LIKE AN ARROW RUNS AWAY FROM YOU

CAST YOUR STONE INTO THE FIRE
NOW FEET DON'T WALK
AND I'M SO TIRED, IT'S TRUE
SO TRUE

WHAT HAVE YOU DONE TO ME, BABY?
OH THESE DAYS JUST BREAK ME
AND NOW I'M WASTED
AND WAKE IN THE MORNING
AND GET UP SCREAMING

AND HERE COMES THE WAVE
HERE COMES THE WAVE
HERE COMES THE WAVE

I LEFT MY LIFE SOMEWHERE BEHIND
MY SCREWED-UP EYES DON'T SEEM TO SHINE
SINCE THE DAY YOU SAID GOODBYE
I JUST CAN'T SEEM TO TRY, IT'S TRUE
SO TRUE

WHAT HAVE YOU DONE TO ME, BABY?
I'M JUST WASTED
AND WAKE IN THE MORNING AND GET UP –

Song ends abruptly. POPPY *pulls herself together and goes.*

Scene Five

1960. HARRY *and* ROSE *enter from the bedroom.*

ROSE. And we haven't even got curtains yet.

HARRY. You can't see owt this high up.

ROSE. You're the devil, you are.

HARRY. But you love me.

ROSE. Like the fool I am. New neighbours and all.

HARRY. They're all at it. Mind you, I went up to see Trev and
Susie on the tenth floor – all she could talk about was the sinks.

ROSE. The sinks?

HARRY. You know, the disposal, the... for the rubbish.

ROSE. Oh, right.

HARRY. It is pretty nifty.

ROSE. If you think you married the kind of woman who can get
excited about waste disposal, you're in for a lifetime of
disappointment.

HARRY. It's a feat of engineering.

ROSE. I'll let you wash up then. (*Beat.*) Aren't you running
late?

HARRY. Trying to get rid of me? You got a fancy man coming
round?

ROSE. That's right. I've got a tea date with Marty Wilde at ten.

HARRY. Oh, I see.

ROSE. He can't wait to see the waste disposal.

HARRY. You're a cruel woman, you are.

ROSE. But you love me. (*Beat.*) I'm having lunch with Carly,
actually. I think she's on a recruitment drive.

HARRY. Well, let her down gently.

ROSE. All sorts going at Coles right now.

HARRY. No need though, is there? Your husband is on track to
be the youngest foreman this city has ever seen, so you can
very politely tell Carly and her perfume counter to go shove it.

ROSE. I never minded working.

HARRY. Besides, you'll have a more important job before too
long.

ROSE. We don't –

HARRY. Can't let anything get in the way of that. Can't be having you on your feet all day.

ROSE. Harry –

HARRY. Won't be like before.

ROSE. It weren't because of that. (*Beat*.) Harry? They never –

HARRY. I'm just saying –

ROSE. That weren't why.

HARRY. I'm not… I'm going to look after you – don't you worry. We're sitting pretty – we're on top of the world.

ROSE. But if we can't… If I –

HARRY (*glancing at his watch*). Right – I really will be late now. What've you done me?

ROSE. One cheese and pickle, one ham and egg.

HARRY. You're a marvel, you are.

ROSE. I know.

A kiss.

HARRY (*on his way towards the door*). Youngest foreman in history – I'm telling you. Can Marty Wilde say that?

ROSE. I'll make sure he knows.

HARRY is almost gone, ROSE coughs. HARRY returns for his jacket, then starts to go again. ROSE coughs. HARRY returns for his sandwiches, starts to go. ROSE coughs a third time.

HARRY. What now?

ROSE pulls HARRY in for a more forceful kiss.

ROSE. Will you miss me?

HARRY. You'll make me late, woman. Now behave.

HARRY finally leaves. Music starts. A microphone appears from somewhere impossible and ROSE sings into it.

Song: 'I'm Looking for Someone to Find Me'

ROSE. WHEN YOU'RE TIRED AND LONELY
AND YOUR HEART HAS NOWHERE TO HEAD
THINK OF ME, I'LL BE THINKING SOMEWHERE
ALL OF THOSE THINGS THAT YOU SAID

DON'T BE CRUEL TO ME
DON'T BE CRUEL TO ME

COS –

ROSE is joined by female backing SINGERS/DANCERS *from the company.*

ROSE/WOMEN. I'M LOOKING FOR SOMEONE TO
FIND ME
I'M LOOKING FOR SOMEONE TO LOVE
I'M HOPING THAT SOMEONE WILL FIND ME
I GOT NO ONE TO LOVE

Other MEN *from the company join in, ready for the day's work. They might sing to the women,* ROSE *at the centre of it all (enjoying the attention). Perhaps this next verse is taken by a Marty Wilde lookalike, conjured from nowhere to serenade her.*

MAN. WHEN YOUR DAYS
ARE PLAGUED BY LONELINESS
YOU GOT NO ONE TO CALL
MY NAME IS HERE IN THE PHONE BOOK
I'LL BE STRAIGHT ROUND TO YOURS

DON'T BE CRUEL TO ME
DON'T BE CRUEL TO ME
COS –

COMPANY. I'M LOOKING FOR SOMEONE TO FIND ME
I'M LOOKING FOR SOMEONE TO LOVE
I'M HOPING THAT SOMEONE WILL FIND ME
I GOT NO ONE TO LOVE, I GOT NO ONE TO LOVE

In 2015, POPPY *appears on her balcony. Her lyric has a more wistful feel.*

POPPY. I'M HOPING THAT SOMEONE WILL FIND ME
   SOMEONE TO CALL MY OWN
   SOMEONE WHO WILL BE KIND TO ME

COMPANY. COS I GOT NO ONE TO LOVE

   ROSE *whistles and suddenly the stage is full of life and*
   bustle. A movement break.

SOLO 1. WHEN YOU'RE FACED WITH LIFE
   THAT AIN'T WORKING
   WHEN YOUR HEART IS HEAVY INSIDE

SOLO 2. WELL, IT'S TIME TO THINK OF LEAVING
   ALL THAT DARKENS YOUR MIND

ROSE/POPPY. DON'T BE CRUEL TO ME
   DON'T BE CRUEL TO ME

   COS –

   Perhaps it's now the end of the workday and HARRY *is back*
   home. He dances with ROSE.

COMPANY. I'M LOOKING FOR SOMEONE TO FIND ME
   I'M LOOKING FOR SOMEONE TO LOVE
   I'M HOPING THAT SOMEONE WILL FIND ME
   I GOT NO ONE TO LOVE

   I'M LOOKING FOR SOMEONE TO FIND ME
   I'M LOOKING FOR SOMEONE TO LOVE
   I'M HOPING THAT SOMEONE WILL FIND ME
   I GOT NO ONE TO LOVE
   I GOT NO ONE TO LOVE

   Song ends. Stage clears. Into –

Scene Six

1989. JOY *is on a walkway outside her flat, glancing nervously over her shoulder. A shout from behind her.*

GARY (*off*). There she is!

> JOY *is rummaging in a backpack, trying to find her keys. She isn't quick enough. Two teenagers,* GARY *and* KEVIN, *cut her off. They're out of breath.*

KEVIN. Why'd you run?

GARY. Not scared, are you? Scared of us?

KEVIN. What's your name?

GARY. 'Ere, my friend asked you a question.

KEVIN. Where they stuck you then? Not on t' paedo wing? (*Tuts.*) Too bad.

GARY (*chuckles*). We'll, uh, have to protect her, won't we?

> *Another shout from off.*

JIMMY (*off*). Oi!

> JIMMY *enters.*

GARY. Alright, Jimmy?

JIMMY. Alright, dickheads. You making friends?

KEVIN. Yeah, we saw her first.

GARY. State of what they're sticking in now. Junkies, prossies, scroungers –

JIMMY. And that's just round your mum's, in't it?

> KEVIN *laughs.*

GARY. Piss off.

JIMMY. Piss off yourself. (*Beat.*) I mean it – both of you. Done the welcome party, so now you can do one.

GARY. Fuck you, Jimmy. You don't even live here no more.

JIMMY. Won't ask again.

A second of stand-off.

KEVIN. Whatever. Leave 'em to it. (*To* JIMMY.) Why d'you even still come round? There's fuck-all here – just look at it. (*To* GARY.) Come on.

GARY *and* KEVIN *go.* JIMMY *turns to* JOY.

JIMMY. You okay?

He makes a move towards her. JOY *flinches.*

I'm not… Do you speak English? You – English?

JOY (*hesitantly*). Yes.

JIMMY. Right. That's the problem then, cos they speak fuck-all of it. Dickheads. Sorry. I'm Jimmy. (*He gestures to himself.*) Jimmy.

JOY. Jimmy?

JIMMY. That's right. And you?

JOY. Joy.

JIMMY. Nice to meet you, Joy. (*Quickly, casually.*) Pay no heed. They're just mardy cos Blades got battered on Sat'day but they'd shit their kegs if you said boo to 'em so it's alreyt. (*Beat.*) What? What's that face in aid of?

JOY. I can't… Your accent, it's –

JIMMY. I've not got an accent.

JOY. Not like the English on the radio.

JIMMY. Ah, well that's cos the BBC are the Bourgeoisie Bastards of Capitalism, and have forsaken their remit to lend a voice to the struggles of the working man. (*Beat.*) Sorry. So you live here, do you? In here?

JOY *nods.*

JIMMY. Nice one. Good place, is this. Used to mi'sen – not any more, but… You'll be reyt. (*Beat.*) I should leave you to it.

JOY (*as if testing the word*). Jimmy?

JIMMY (*grins*). That's right. (*Beat.*) I could check in on you, if
   you like? Make sure you're getting no bother. Don't… You
   don't have to answer – maybe can't answer, but I will, if
   that's okay? (*Beat.*) Okay. Can you get in? Got a key?

   JOY *has now found her key – she produces it.*

JOY. Yes.

JIMMY. Good. Right, I guess I'll be seeing you around. Ta-ra
   now.

JOY. Ta-ra.

   JIMMY *goes.* JOY *remains onstage.* POPPY *appears on the
   balcony and sings.*

Song: 'I'm Looking for Someone to Find Me' (Reprise)

POPPY. I'M HOPING THAT SOMEONE WILL FIND ME
   SOMEONE TO CALL MY OWN
   SOMEONE WHO WILL BE KIND TO ME
   COS I GOT NO ONE IN THIS WORLD OR THIS LIFE
   I NEED SOMEONE TO LOVE
   I NEED SOMEONE TO LOVE
   I NEED SOMETHING TO LOVE

Scene Seven

A split scene. We begin in 1989. JOY *is being quizzed by*
GRACE *at the kitchen table. We will also move between*
HARRY *and* ROSE *having dinner in 1960, and* POPPY *having
dinner with her work friend* MARCUS *in 2015.*

GRACE. Who was he?

JOY. Just a boy.

GRACE. You shouldn't be talking to boys.

JOY. He saved me.

GRACE. Even so –

JOY. His name is Jimmy. He's my friend.

GRACE. I don't want you making that sort of friend.

JOY. You haven't even met him!

GRACE. I don't want you to see him again.

JOY. But –

GRACE. And that's an end to it.

JOY. You're not my mother.

GRACE (*refusing to rise to this*). If I was your mother you'd have been raised not to answer back. Now set the table, please.

2015. Doorbell rings. POPPY *lets in* MARCUS, *thirties, local, her slightly hipster workmate.*

POPPY. Hi!

MARCUS. Hey! This is swish.

POPPY. I know, right? Come in. Coat anywhere. What can I…? I've got white wine in the fridge, or a G&T? A friend sent me this bottle of Yorkshire Tea gin as a joke, and it's surprisingly not awful.

MARCUS. Oh, well now you've sold it.

POPPY. Yeah? It's nice, I promise. (*She starts making drinks.*) Y'know I seem to have become one of those people who people buy gin for, which is fine, which is *nice*, but I have been trying to cut back on… well, drinking alone anyway.

MARCUS. Always happy to enable.

POPPY. Thanks. You find me okay?

MARCUS. You're hard to miss. Local landmark, you know.

POPPY. Right.

MARCUS. People used to come from miles around to chuck themselves off here.

POPPY. Terrific.

MARCUS. Sorry, just this place was… There was a time –

POPPY. Oh, I know. Done my research – watched the documentary, got the picture book –

MARCUS. Bought the T-shirt?

POPPY. Something like that, yeah. (*Handing him a drink.*) Here.

MARCUS. Cheers.

POPPY. Cheers.

1960. HARRY *enters*.

HARRY. Evening!

2015.

POPPY (*to* MARCUS). Do you want the tour?

POPPY *and* MARCUS *go. 1960*. ROSE *hands* HARRY *a glass of beer.*

HARRY. Ta very much.

ROSE. How was it?

HARRY. Y'know. Hot and heavy. Same old same old.

ROSE. Sounds like my afternoon with Marty.

HARRY. Does it now? Something smells good.

ROSE. Shepherd's pie.

HARRY. Heaven.

ROSE. Won't be long. I'll get the veg on now.

HARRY. How was she then?

ROSE. You've got time to clean up if you like.

HARRY. Oh?

ROSE. If you want. Scrape some of that muck off.

HARRY. Right.

Back to 1989.

GRACE. Don't sulk, Joy.

1960.

HARRY. Won't be a minute.

HARRY *goes. Back to 1989.*

GRACE. I'm only trying to protect you.

JOY. That's what he was doing! He isn't like the others. He is the only one here who doesn't hate us.

GRACE. Nobody hates us.

JOY. They do. And do you know what they shout at me? 'Go home – why don't you go home?' What should I tell them?

GRACE. Nothing. You say nothing to people like that.

GEORGE *enters.*

JOY. They hate us and I hate them. I hate the smell and the cold and the rain –

GRACE. Then be grateful for the roof over your head that keeps it out.

GEORGE (*to* GRACE). Have you heard?

JOY. Heard what?

GEORGE. Oh, I… (*He changes what he was about to say.*) I heard it might snow tonight. Imagine that – our first snow.

GRACE. It's okay. She should know. Yes, it was on the radio.

JOY. What was?

GEORGE. Taylor's invasion is underway. They're fighting in Nimba County.

JOY (*quietly*). Oh.

GEORGE (*quickly*). But they didn't come through Guinea. Guinea is still –

GRACE (*still to* JOY). Do you see? See why we have to stay here, where it's safe?

JOY. It doesn't feel safe.

GRACE. It is – as long as the door stays locked.

JOY. Like a prison.

GEORGE. Like a castle – an Englishman's home is his castle – or so they say.

JOY. But we are not English.

GRACE. That's enough. (*Beat.*) We all just need to eat something.

Back in 2015, POPPY *and* MARCUS *return.*

POPPY. You don't have any allergies, do you? I went veggie because I thought that was safest. It's an Ottolenghi aubergine thing. Sort of Middle Eastern.

MARCUS. Fancy.

POPPY. Did you know you can get fresh turmeric root in the market here?

MARCUS. I did not.

POPPY. Crazy. Who needs Ocado?

MARCUS. No one. Fundamentally.

POPPY. Fair enough.

MARCUS. So how're you settling in so far?

POPPY. I don't know – but I'm trying, I really am. You know I lived in London for twelve years and I never knew the name of a single neighbour. Not this time. I'm going to make the people in this building love me. I've been knocking on doors – baked biscuits, even –

MARCUS. Really?

POPPY. Uh-huh. Gluten-free, entirely inedible biscuits. But it's a start. I want to learn a bit of that fabled northern hospitality.

MARCUS. So is that why you left London?

POPPY. Oh no, that was… Ugh. Okay. No, that is a long and complicated story that definitely requires more gin.

MARCUS. Someone break your heart?

POPPY. Oh. Okay. Really short story then.

Timelines cross for a moment.

GRACE. George, can you help?

ROSE (*calling off*). Harry! I'm serving!

POPPY. Do you want another?

1960. HARRY *returns*.

ROSE. Bit more human?

HARRY. A bit. So go on then – how was Our Lady of Perpetual Fragrance?

ROSE. Good – she was good. Barely talked shop at all.

HARRY. Oh?

ROSE. Yeah. She, um, she had other news. (*Beat.*) She's expecting again.

HARRY. Oh, right.

ROSE. Yeah.

HARRY. Number four. Jesus. Must be something in the water.

ROSE. I don't think it was planned, but –

HARRY. Right.

ROSE. And their Eddie starts school this autumn, so that'll take some pressure off.

HARRY. School? No, it's… Has it been that long?

ROSE. It has, yeah.

A silence.

HARRY. Well. Four. I don't envy them that, I must say.

ROSE. No. (*Beat.*) Sit yourself down – I'll dish up.

HARRY. Cracking.

1989, GRACE brings bowls of stew to the table.

GRACE. Sorry if it's bland. I still don't know where to find pepper.

GEORGE. Thank you.

GRACE. I don't think the English season anything.

GEORGE nudges JOY.

JOY. Thank you, Auntie.

GEORGE *(trying to fill a silence)*. I think… I think all Liberia knew this was coming. Now it can be over quickly. The sooner it's over the sooner we go back. I think… I think…

GRACE. I think let's all just eat our dinner.

JOY. I'm not hungry.

In 2015, a timer bleeps.

POPPY. Here we go!

1989.

JOY. How will we know when it's safe?

GRACE. We'll know. Our parents will write.

JOY. And then we'll find mine, in Guinea?

GEORGE. Yes.

JOY. And Guinea is safe?

GRACE. Joy! Please just stop asking questions for two seconds and eat! *(Beat – she calms.)* Oh, I did get something – from a shop near the market.

GRACE turns back to the counter. We move back to 2015.

MARCUS. Almost forgot. I got you a house-warming present.

MARCUS produces a bottle of Henderson's Relish wrapped in tissue paper, which he brought with him. This single bottle will be passed between all timelines.

POPPY. You didn't have to. (*Opening it*.) Oh – I've heard of this. Henderson's Relish?

MARCUS. Another step in your cultural education. The 'H' is silent.

GRACE *takes the bottle and puts it on the table*.

GEORGE. What is this?

GRACE. I have no idea, but it is very important to them.

GEORGE (*sniffing the bottle*). It smells like… What is that smell? (*To* JOY.) Try it.

JOY *wrinkles her nose*.

GRACE. Well I will.

POPPY. Do you think it goes with slow-baked aubergine?

MARCUS. It goes with anything – trust.

POPPY *shrugs. The bottle is now passed between timelines as all liberally add Henderson's Relish to their plates and taste. A moment of fleeting contentment*.

HARRY. Perfect.

GRACE. That is… Yes. I like it. Joy?

JOY (*clearly won over*). It's okay.

POPPY. So it's just Worcestershire sauce?

MARCUS (*firmly*). No. Uh-uh. Never say that again.

POPPY. Okay.

HARRY (*to* ROSE). Pass the Hendo's.

GEORGE. There must be other Africans here – they have small-small pepper after all.

ROSE. I don't know how you can taste anything else.

HARRY. I don't know why you'd want to.

ROSE (*mock offended*). Thank you very much.

GRACE (*to* JOY). You want some more?

POPPY. It's... interesting. Fruity. Hmm.

MARCUS. And gluten free.

POPPY. Alright, I'm convinced.

MARCUS. Good. We'll make a local of you yet.

POPPY. Can I ask a question? Does Karen hate me – Karen in finance?

MARCUS. Why would you say that?

POPPY. Because of everything she's ever said to me.

MARCUS. No, she's just... it's not... Isn't great with outsiders. She'll come round.

HARRY (*to* ROSE). You're a marvel. Thank you.

ROSE. You're welcome.

POPPY (*to* MARCUS). Well, thank you for reaching out. Honestly. I needed it.

We settle in 1989 for a moment. JOY *is now by the sink.* GRACE *talks to* GEORGE.

GRACE. You hear her call me 'Auntie'? I didn't think I'd be Auntie so soon. (*Beat.*) She met a boy today.

GEORGE (*teasing*). Don't worry, sister, you will too.

GRACE *bats at* GEORGE. *He grins and moves over to* JOY.

(*To* JOY.) Hey – you know what else I learnt today? I was walking on the hill just behind us – you know what they call it? Skye Edge. You're living at the edge of the sky – now can any of your friends say that?

JOY (*quietly*). No.

GEORGE. And how many have a view like this one? How many have ever tasted '*Henderson's Relish*'? No one I know. I think there are good things here, if we go looking for them.

JOY. It doesn't feel like a castle.

GEORGE. I know.

JOY. I'm scared.

GEORGE. I know. So am I. All adventures are scary. But all this is ours now – this is where we belong. (*Beat*.) Now go help wash up.

Back to 1960.

HARRY (*to* ROSE). I'd do anything for you, you know that?

ROSE. What's come over you? Soppy sod.

HARRY. I mean it – I'm going to give you everything. I promise.

Music starts. In 2015 POPPY *is seeing* MARCUS *out.*

MARCUS. You know what, I think the fresh turmeric made all the difference.

POPPY. Shut up! Get home safe – I'll see you Monday.

MARCUS. Will do. Keep knocking on doors, eh?

MARCUS goes. In 1989, GEORGE *watches* JOY *from across the room.*

Song: 'Tonight the Streets Are Ours'

As GEORGE *sings we see the three timelines settling into their routines.* POPPY *and* JOY *both become more comfortable.* HARRY *and* ROSE *grow closer.* GEORGE *oversees it all.*

GEORGE. DO YOU KNOW WHY
  YOU GOT FEELINGS IN YOUR HEART?
  DON'T LET FEAR OF FEELING FOOL YOU
  WHAT YOU SEE SETS YOU APART
  AND THERE'S NOTHING HERE TO BIND YOU
  IT'S NO WAY FOR LIFE TO START

  DO YOU KNOW THAT
  TONIGHT THE STREETS ARE OURS?
  TONIGHT THE STREETS ARE OURS
  THESE LIGHTS IN OUR HEARTS THEY TELL NO LIES

  SOME PEOPLE THEY GOT NOTHING IN THEIR SOULS
  AND THEY MAKE OUR TVS BLIND US

FROM OUR VISION AND OUR GOALS
OH, THE TRIGGER OF TIME IT TRICKS YOU
SO YOU HAVE NO WAY TO GROW

BUT DO YOU KNOW THAT
TONIGHT THE STREETS ARE OURS
TONIGHT THE STREETS ARE OURS
THESE LIGHTS IN OUR HEARTS THEY TELL NO LIES

The full COMPANY *sing the bridge.*

COMPANY. AND NO ONE ELSE CAN HAUNT ME
THE WAY THAT YOU CAN HAUNT ME
I NEED TO KNOW YOU WANT ME
I COULDN'T BE WITHOUT YOU
AND THE LIGHT THAT SHINES AROUND YOU

NO NOTHING EVER MATTERED MORE
THAN NOT DOUBTING
THAT TONIGHT THE STREETS ARE OURS

GEORGE *watches* HARRY *and* ROSE.

GEORGE. DO YOU KNOW HOW
TO KILL LONELINESS AT LAST?
OH, THERE'S SO MUCH THERE TO HEAL, DEAR
AND MAKE TEARSTAINS OF THE PAST

BUT DO YOU KNOW THAT
TONIGHT THE STREETS ARE OURS
TONIGHT THE STREETS ARE OURS

All timelines join in. It's triumphant.

COMPANY. AND THESE LIGHTS
IN OUR STREETS ARE OURS
TONIGHT THE STREETS ARE OURS
THESE LIGHTS IN OUR HEARTS THEY TELL NO LIES

Song ends. Into –

ACT TWO

*At the top of the act, we see our first big jump forward in time.
1960 skips on to 1979, 1989 to 1992, and 2015 to 2017. We
should hit this with a bit of a clunk – the optimism we've just
witnessed suddenly hitting a brick wall.*

*We're also now in three election years. Ideally we might see
some Labour paraphernalia in 1979 and 1992. In 2017,* POPPY
sticks a Lib Dem poster on her fridge.

Scene One

CONNIE *appears.*

CONNIE. Years pass when you're not looking.
    Rot sets in
    And other things too
    When life catches in the gears of the waste disposal
    And grinds, and grinds, and grinds
    Shine's worn off – cracks starting to show.
    No matter though – we're made of stronger stuff.
    And as it goes, tonight's election night –
    So who knows what might change?
    We vote for rocks and hard places
    Expectations at an all-time low
    Still, things can't stay the same.

A brief moment in 2017. POPPY *with* MARCUS. *He clocks
her poster.*

MARCUS. Wouldn't get your hopes up. Still redder than Lenin
    on a Routemaster round here.

POPPY. It's not the winning, it's the taking part that counts.

MARCUS. That is such a Lib Dem thing to say. (*Beat.*) I saw
    someone's smashed the sign again.

POPPY. Hmm?

MARCUS. The 'I love you'.

POPPY. Oh yeah, barely lasted a week this time.

MARCUS. And speaking of broken hearts –

POPPY. Jesus, how long have you been preparing that?

MARCUS. I'm just worried about you. If you don't shag something soon, you're going to forget how.

POPPY. Leave me alone or I'll report you to HR.

MARCUS. It's been, what – two years?

POPPY. It's complicated.

MARCUS. Just let me set you up. I know your ex was a total psycho, but –

POPPY. No, don't say that. I can say that, you can't.

MARCUS. But are you still getting the messages?

POPPY. It isn't… Nikki isn't… It's all under control. I'm fine.

MARCUS. If you say so. (*Beat.*) Oh, and Karen's birthday on Tuesday – very partial to a lemon drizzle, so I'm told.

POPPY. Great – I'm on it.

Moment ends. POPPY *and* MARCUS *exit and* CONNIE *comes forward again. It's 1992.*

CONNIE. So life goes on
We learn how to survive
These balconies like battlements in the right light
A castle built of streets in the sky
Election number two,
And hope fizzes like sherbet, tingling on your tongue –
This one's gonna get us back on track.
Love blossoms in the most unlikely places
Love amongst the piss-smelling walkways
The world's most effective air freshener
Love will save us
Or at least see us through another night.

JOY (*now seventeen*) *is leaving the flat.* GRACE *sees her off.*

GRACE. I want you home before dark. You heard what happened to that boy last week –

JOY. I know.

GRACE. Within an inch of his life. Animals. While I'm out this evening I want the door bolted the whole time.

JOY. Couldn't I go out too, seeing as you're – ?

GRACE (*with just a hint of warning*). Joy –

JOY. If it's safe for you –

GRACE. It isn't the same. I am an election observer – I am participating in the democratic process – that is –

JOY. I know, but –

GRACE. No buts. Be patient. Be safe. (*Checks her watch.*) And don't be late for school.

JOY *starts to go.* GRACE *holds out her keys.*

Hey, little genius – forgetting something? Who are you walking with?

JOY (*trying to hide a smile*). Just a friend. (*Beat.*) I'll be straight home.

JOY *kisses* GRACE *on the cheek and goes.* GRACE *exits. We're moving into 1979.*

CONNIE. All grown up. Almost.
And all her hopes are now pinned to this place
Unlikely as it sounds
For now almost content.
Not with election three,
Where endless winter births a bitter spring
Stomachs knot at what the night might bring
But life can still surprise us, even here –

1979. HARRY, ROSE *and their eight-year-old son* JAMES *now visible. It's morning here too.* JAMES *is being prepared for school,* HARRY *about to leave for work.*

Ten years of trying, then he arrives
A miracle imperfectly timed
A blessing and a curse.
Another mouth. An anchor. A weight.
Not that you'd have it any other way.
So you crack on, cut back, make do,
Because tomorrow is another day.

CONNIE *goes*.

Scene Two

Still in 1979. HARRY, ROSE *and* JAMES.

ROSE. Right – both got your lunches? Both got your scarves?

JAMES. Yes.

HARRY. Yes, Mum.

ROSE. And keep out of trouble, the pair of you.

HARRY. We'll see.

JAMES (*reciting what he's learnt by rote*). Sometimes it falls to the working man to take up arms and fight for those inalienable rights that others take for granted.

ROSE. Is that so?

HARRY. Not bad, that, is it? (*To* JAMES.) And what else?

JAMES. Sometimes you've got to give the bastards a hiding.

HARRY (*to* ROSE). Well, he didn't learn that from me.

ROSE. Behave. (*To* JAMES.) Done your teeth?

JAMES *nods, mouth firmly closed*.

Show me.

JAMES *turns away*.

Right – bathroom – do 'em quick, before you're late.

JAMES *goes off, sulking slightly.*

Cheeky beggar. Can't think who he gets it from.

HARRY *smirks.*

He'll not be in those boots long. Toes poking through already.

HARRY. Right.

ROSE. I'll ask our Linda if she's got owt for him. Or your Evie might.

HARRY. No need.

ROSE. No bother. They race through 'em at this age.

HARRY. I'll sort it.

ROSE. We both grew up in hand-me-downs –

HARRY (*firmly*). Not him. Not him, or what's the point in…? I'll sort it. Two new pair by end o't' week. Just let me know what you need.

ROSE. Okay. (*Beat.*) And I'll be knocking on some doors with Barbara this afternoon, but I should still be home before you.

HARRY. Might be late. I'll have some calls to make for the union.

ROSE. There's a phone here.

HARRY. They've tapped the phones here.

ROSE. They haven't –

HARRY. Take no chances, on a night like tonight.

ROSE. You'll be in The George then?

HARRY (*raising his voice, just a little*). I'll be working, I'll be… Do you know what's at stake here? You think it's bad now? We've seen nothing – just you wait till –

He spots JAMES has just returned. He stops himself.

Not too late, I promise. (*To* JAMES.) Be good. Listen to your mother.

HARRY *kisses* ROSE *and goes*.

ROSE (*to* JAMES). All clean?

JAMES *bares his teeth at* ROSE.

Alright then, let's get you gone too. Chop-chop.

JAMES. Mum?

ROSE. Yes?

JAMES. Will I be a steel man like Dad when I'm older?

ROSE. Is that what you want?

JAMES. I'd rather be an astronaut.

ROSE. Is that right?

JAMES. I'll be the first man on Mars. I'll go further than anyone ever has before.

ROSE. Well, you can't build a spaceship without steel.

JAMES (*wide-eyed*). Does Dad build spaceships?

ROSE. Might do.

JAMES. Mum?

ROSE. Yes?

JAMES. Why's he always angry?

ROSE. He's not.

JAMES. He is.

ROSE. It isn't… It's just work – it's a difficult time.

JAMES. Because of the spaceships?

ROSE. That's right. Not building as many spaceships as they used to. But don't you worry. Spaceships, trucks, the trains you watch coming and going from the window – it's all steel. People will always need him.

JAMES. Okay.

ROSE. Right. Got everything?

JAMES *nods.*

Good lad. Let's go.

JAMES. Race you!

JAMES *picks up a satchel and dashes off.*

ROSE. No running! James! James!

ROSE *follows. Immediately into –*

Scene Three

As young JAMES disappears off one way, older JIMMY (now twenty-one) appears in 1992, perhaps dressed similarly enough to help us make the connection. JOY enters from another direction. She has schoolbooks/folders with her. Her calls might overlap with ROSE's.

JOY. Jimmy! Over here!

JIMMY. Alright?

JOY (*in her best Yorkshire*). Ay up, duck.

JIMMY. Very good.

JOY. You mean 'reet gradely'.

JIMMY. Who taught you that?

JOY. I have lots of teachers.

JIMMY. Oh aye. Trying to make me jealous?

JOY. I'm a star pupil.

JIMMY. Don't doubt it. Here – got you something.

JOY *offers her cheek for a kiss, but* JIMMY *produces a flower instead, slightly wilted. She's surprised, but likes it.*

JOY. Oh. Thank you.

JIMMY. And what've you got for me?

JOY. You can have quadratic equations, the circulatory system or William Blake.

JIMMY. Ooh, Blake – I know him. 'Jerusalem', right? Dark Satanic Mills – visions of a socialist utopia once the workers have risen up and grasped the means of production.

JOY. Er, no – it's about –

JIMMY. Yes! 'I will not cease from Mental Fight, nor shall my sword sleep in my hand' –

JOY. Yes, but –

JIMMY. So it means there's a fight coming, yeah, and it's going to be mental, but we've got to tool up, keep the faith, and Neil Kinnock's gonna lead us all in glorious revolution.

JOY (*laughing*). You are no help.

JIMMY. I'm telling you – William Blake – proper comrade.

JOY. Do you want me to pass these exams?

JIMMY. What do doctors need to know about poetry for anyway?

JOY. I want to know about everything.

JIMMY. Just showing off, you are. Too smart for this place. Too smart for me.

JOY. Don't say that.

JIMMY. Nah, I mean it. You'll not stop here long, will you? No way.

JOY. Where else would I go?

JIMMY. Right. No, just cos you always said… Thought you wanted to get home, as soon as they stopped fighting.

JOY. This is home. (*Beat*.) I don't think there's much to go back to.

JIMMY. Oh. (*Beat*.) Listen. Gotta tell you something.

JOY. You can tell me anything.

JIMMY. I've been offered a job.

JOY. That's good. That's brilliant.

JIMMY. Yeah, it's… My uncle found me something, and it pays well – really well, for what it is. Thing is… It's an oil rig. Um. North Sea. Middle of nowhere.

JOY. North Sea?

JIMMY. Yeah. Months at a time you're gone, and…

JOY. You're leaving?

JIMMY. Wish I weren't, but – (*Off her look*.) Joy, there's just nothing for me here.

JOY. I'm here.

JIMMY. I'm not –

JOY. And you have been saying for weeks – months – tonight, everything changes. Neil Kinnock – revolution – Jerusalem! 'We're alright!'

JIMMY. I know, but –

JOY. It's going to be alright.

JIMMY. And it will be – it will for you, but… There's a part of this city that's gone, and whatever happens I don't think it's coming back. I've not had a sniff of work for months. I've gotta think about Mum, looking after her, and –

JOY. You still haven't taken me dancing. You promised –

JIMMY. And that's tricky, in't it, when your Grace don't let you out the flat.

JOY. It'll change when I'm eighteen – only a few months.

JIMMY. And then you'll have the pick of the city – pick of the world. I mean it. You can go anywhere. Just stay on't right side of Pennines. And not Leeds – Leeds are dickheads.

JOY. Don't joke about this –

JIMMY. I'm not. Even if you do stay here, how's it gonna work? You're gonna be a doctor saving lives, in some big old stone house in Fulwood, oak tree in the garden, BMW in the drive, eating fucking lobsters and Viennetta, so... so... We don't fit, do we? And we've not really done owt yet –

JOY. We –

JIMMY. Kissing's not... I just reckon it's best.

JOY. Don't do this. Let's talk about this.

JIMMY. You'll be late. Can't have that.

JOY. Tonight then. Come over tonight. Grace will be out – we can... You don't want this. And things will change – after tonight, everything will change. Promise me.

JIMMY. We should get you going. Come on.

    JIMMY *goes,* JOY *follows.*

Scene Four

2017. Late afternoon/early evening. NIKKI *appears at a microphone.*

Song: 'Open Up Your Door'

NIKKI. OPEN UP YOUR DOOR
   I CAN'T SEE YOUR FACE NO MORE
   LOVE IS SO HARD TO FIND
   AND EVEN HARDER TO DEFINE

   OH, OPEN UP YOUR DOOR
   COS WE'VE TIME TO GIVE

AND I'M FEELING IT SO MUCH MORE
OPEN UP THE DOOR
OPEN UP YOUR DOOR

OPEN UP THE DOOR
I CAN'T HEAR YOUR VOICE NO MORE
I JUST WANT TO MAKE YOU SMILE
MAYBE STAY WITH YOU AWHILE

OH, OPEN UP YOUR DOOR
COS WE'VE TIME TO GIVE
AND MY FEELINGS AREN'T SO OBSCURE
OPEN UP THE DOOR
OPEN UP YOUR DOOR

SO OPEN UP THE DOOR
COS WE'VE TIME TO GIVE
AND I'M FEELING IT SO MUCH MORE
OPEN UP YOUR DOOR
OH, OPEN UP YOUR DOOR

LOVE IS SO HARD TO FIND
AND EVEN HARDER TO DEFINE

OH, OPEN UP YOUR DOOR
AND I'VE NEVER BEEN SO SURE
OH, OPEN UP YOUR DOOR
OPEN UP YOUR DOOR!

CONNIE *appears, having just shown* NIKKI *round a flat.*

CONNIE. So what do you think?

NIKKI. Yeah. They're just *nice*, aren't they? I wasn't really expecting… I don't know what I was expecting actually.

CONNIE. It's a top-end job – been a lot of interest. Did you have any other questions?

NIKKI. Um, one thing – I read about a tent city – a homeless city, on the estate.

CONNIE. Oh. Yes, there was. Not any more.

NIKKI. Right. (*Beat.*) Where did they go to?

CONNIE. I'm not sure.

NIKKI. Where did they all go – all the people who used to live here – back before?

CONNIE. They… Uh. I'm not –

NIKKI. Are you not allowed to tell me?

CONNIE. No! The estate just… mostly it just emptied out, over time, long before anyone was talking about redevelopment. This wasn't somewhere people wanted to live. But that's all changed now.

NIKKI. I see.

CONNIE. Anything else?

NIKKI. Will you marry me?

CONNIE. I'm sorry?

NIKKI. The sign on the bridge?

CONNIE. Oh, right! Uh, yes, it's… It was graffiti back in the day – became a bit iconic, you could see it from everywhere – then when they were doing the refurb they went over it in neon.

NIKKI. And did they get married?

CONNIE. Uh. No, I'm afraid not. It's quite a sad story actually, but… I don't think she appreciated the gesture.

NIKKI. Right. (*Beat.*) Is it alright if I stay up here for a minute, take some pictures of the view? Gorgeous in this light. I can see myself down.

CONNIE. Sure – and you've got my number, if you think of anything.

NIKKI. Yep. Great, thanks.

CONNIE *goes.* NIKKI *looks around, takes her phone out, consults it. She opens up her backpack, maybe pulls out a bedraggled bunch of flowers/battered chocolates/wine. She's psyching herself up for something. She checks her phone again.*

(*To herself, practising.*) Hey. Hi. So I was… I was passing
through, and… Hey. You look well, you look… Hi, fancy
seeing… Urgh!

She is about to knock on the door when POPPY *rounds the
corner and they find themselves face to face.*

Hey.

POPPY. No – oh no –

NIKKI. I was just, uh –

POPPY. What the…?

NIKKI. Please. I stayed away as long as I could, genuinely –

POPPY. What the hell, Nikki?

NIKKI. But you never answered by calls, and –

POPPY. How did you get up here? Who let you in?

NIKKI. Um. Flat viewing. I organised a viewing of another flat.
They're nice, aren't they? Didn't think they'd be this nice.
Well done.

POPPY. How do you know where I live?

NIKKI. Your dad, uh, he posted a load of pictures of… um, on
Facebook.

POPPY. Why are you still Facebook friends with my dad?

NIKKI. He just never unfriended me, so…

POPPY. You can't be here.

NIKKI. I only want to talk.

POPPY. And I think I've made it pretty clear that I don't, so –

NIKKI. I'm dying, Poppy.

Beat.

POPPY. What?

NIKKI (*now quickly*). Okay, no, that isn't true. I shouldn't have
said that. That is a bad lie and I apologise, but… but I did

think I was. I found a lump – I thought I'd found a lump, and I hadn't, it was actually nothing, but I did legitimately think I was dying for… for like a good few days, and it really made me think – what if I died without ever seeing you again, and –

POPPY. But you're not dying.

NIKKI. We're all dying, Pops.

POPPY. But there's nothing – ?

NIKKI. I think you're missing the point of the story.

POPPY. You're unbelievable.

NIKKI. Just five minutes.

POPPY. I can't.

NIKKI. Why not?

POPPY. I… I'm going pamphleting, actually.

NIKKI. Oh, come on, Pops, that's a lost cause. You know we're all fucked.

POPPY. Typical. Typical selfish Nikki, always –

NIKKI. Sorry! Please, just… hold on, wait – wait –

   NIKKI *starts searching in her pockets for a scrap of paper.*

POPPY. What're you doing?

NIKKI. I want to read you my vows.

POPPY. Jesus Christ.

NIKKI. I love you – will you marry me?

POPPY. Go. Now.

NIKKI. We were meant to be getting married, Pops.

POPPY. We were! Yes, we were, and then you fucked my boss, Nikki!

NIKKI. It wasn't like that.

POPPY. Wasn't it? (*Beat.*) That's what I thought.

POPPY *steps inside her flat.*

NIKKI. Poppy! Pops! Come on! Just five minutes! Please!

The music strikes up again.

OPEN UP YOUR DOOR
OH, OPEN UP YOUR DOOR

LOVE IS SO HARD TO FIND
AND EVEN HARDER TO DEFINE

OH, OPEN UP YOUR DOOR
AND I'VE NEVER BEEN SO SURE
OH, OPEN UP YOUR DOOR
OPEN UP YOUR DOOR!

The door opens. POPPY *steps outside again, handing a wodge of pamphlets to* NIKKI.

POPPY. Five minutes. But you're giving out these.

POPPY *strides off.* NIKKI *smiles and follows.*

Scene Five

1979. Late evening. HARRY *is prowling outside the flat. He's drunk and not doing a great job of hiding it.*

Song: 'My Little Treasures'

HARRY. MY LITTLE TREASURES
I KEEP CLOSE TO ME
THEY GIVE ME SO MUCH PLEASURE
AND SOME COMPANY

Inside the flat, ROSE *enters in a nightdress.*

COLD BEER IN WARM PLACES
HEARTBREAK IN OLD FACES

JAMES *enters and joins* ROSE *on the sofa.*

WITH MY LITTLE TREASURES
YOU'RE MORE THAN OLD BONES
IN SOME SMALLER MEASURE
YOU'RE NEVER ALONE

WARM BEER IN COLD PLACES
WHISKEY-GLASS STORM-CHASERS

LOOK AT ALL THESE STARS
LOOK AT ALL THESE STARS
THERE I DO BELIEVE
IS JUPITER AND MARS
LOOK AT ALL THESE STARS
LOOK AT ALL THESE STARS
HOW DID WE EVER GET SO FAR FROM HERE?

HARRY *steps inside, waking* JAMES *up*.

JAMES. Dad!

ROSE. So you're home.

HARRY. What're you doing up at this hour?

ROSE. We could ask you the same.

JAMES. Wanted to see you.

HARRY. Well, you have now, so –

JAMES. Were you working late on your rocket ship?

HARRY. What's that?

ROSE (*to* JAMES). Come on now – bed.

JAMES. I'm not tired now.

ROSE. Well, I am. I'll tuck you in in a minute.

JAMES *goes*.

How's the mood at the union?

HARRY. Don't. Don't even… That woman has no idea –

ROSE. Polls have been wrong before, and even, even if –

HARRY. No idea. It's ours, this city, this country – we built it. But does she care about…? Where's the understanding? Where's the gratitude?

ROSE. We were born into worse.

HARRY. This is different.

ROSE. We'll survive.

HARRY. No –

ROSE. Yes. Always made our own luck – and God knows Jim Callaghan's been no saint. We'll push back. If you have to strike, you'll strike –

HARRY. Stop it –

ROSE. No surrender. Steel's been pushed around for too long –

HARRY. It's not –

ROSE. And women'll step up too. We've done it before, we'll do it again –

HARRY grabs ROSE forcefully. He might shake her, or hold her face.

HARRY. Stop it! Stop it! Stop, just… You can't fix this.

ROSE. Harry, you're hurting me.

HARRY. I'm the one who'll fix it.

ROSE. Okay.

HARRY. I still matter. This city still needs me.

ROSE. Of course we do.

He lets her go. He shrinks to half his size.

HARRY. I… I didn't…

ROSE. I know. (*Beat.*) Night's young – could still turn around. (*Beat.*) Come to bed soon.

HARRY nods. He remembers something.

HARRY. Rocket ship?

ROSE. You're building a stainless-steel spaceship. Long story.

HARRY. One way out, I guess. (*Beat*.) Go on.

>ROSE *musters a smile and goes*. HARRY *steps out onto the balcony. Song continues –*

COMPANY. LONELY EYES THINK OF YOU FOR AN AGE
>AND FOR A TIME TO TELL THE TRUTH
>OH IT GETS STRANGE

HARRY/COMPANY. THE YOUNGER I COULD NOT
>   FOLLOW YOU
>THE OLDER I MISREMEMBERS YOUTH
>AND FOR A WHILE I WILL DRINK TO YOU
>AND FILL MY CUP WITH RAGE

>MY LITTLE TREASURES
>I KEEP CLOSE TO ME
>COLD BEER IN WARM PLACES
>WHISKEY-GLASS STORM-CHASERS

>LOOK AT ALL THESE STARS
>LOOK AT ALL THESE STARS

>THERE I DO BELIEVE IS
>JUPITER AND MARS
>LOOK AT ALL THESE STARS
>LOOK AT ALL THESE STARS
>HOW DID WE EVER GET SO FAR FROM THERE?
>FROM THERE?

>MY LITTLE TREASURES
>I KEEP CLOSE TO ME

>HARRY *finishes his drink, looking out across the city.*

Scene Six

1992. JOY, GRACE *and* GEORGE. GRACE *is on her way out.*

GRACE. Locked and bolted – the whole time I'm gone.

GEORGE. It'll be fine, I promise.

JOY. You know every other girl my age is allowed out after dark, allowed to go dancing, allowed a life –

GRACE. Then heaven help those girls.

JOY. But you can go? Go enjoy yourself – enjoy your freedom.

GRACE. For the last time! It isn't about '*enjoy*'! This is a solemn duty, not a… a dance hall.

JOY. My parents would want me to be happy. If my mama knew how you keep me prisoner – locked up like a princess in a tower –

GRACE. Then go tell her, okay, princess? When she comes back you tell her what a tyrant I've been, and I will say 'here – take your daughter back – take this child I never asked for – '

GEORGE. Grace –

GRACE. 'Take this *life* I never asked for,' but until then… There is no one coming to save us. Not after all this time. We are all we have. This is all we have. Only this.

JOY *can't respond to this, and storms off to her bedroom.*

GEORGE (*after her*). Joy – don't –

GRACE. Leave her. I can't keep doing this. (*Calling off to* JOY.) I'm locking you in.

GRACE *goes out and* GEORGE *goes off the way Joy left.*

Scene Seven

2017. POPPY *and* NIKKI *come back inside the flat.*

NIKKI. That's better. Chilly, isn't it?

POPPY. You'll have a train to catch.

NIKKI (*putting down pamphlets*). Not the warmest reception to these, either. (*Looking around.*) Oh, it's nice inside too. Much nicer than the one they showed me. They can be a bit soulless at first, can't they?

POPPY. Why did you come here?

NIKKI. I bet it's a good investment though. That's what the woman said. Didn't trust her. You know they kicked them out, the last few families who lived here? I was reading up. They had to evict them. But they are lovely now.

POPPY. What are you doing here? Seriously.

NIKKI. I'm… I'm getting to that, I'm building up to that. I just… I, uh, I spoke to Victor, actually. I don't know if you know this, but Fiona's moved on, um, she's in the Cardiff office now, so he needs a new Head of Digital.

POPPY. Right.

NIKKI. Yours, if you want it. Said he'd double whatever you're on here.

POPPY. So – so what? So you're here to make a job offer?

NIKKI. No. I'm here to bring you home.

POPPY. I am home.

NIKKI. No you're not. I know places like this, and this is not your home. (*Glancing around.*) Do you bake now? Is it that bad? Have they made you a baker?

POPPY. It's calming, actually.

NIKKI. Do you bring in brownies for staff meetings? Have you joined a ramblers' club? Tell me, quite honestly, if I look in your wardrobe right now will I find a jumper with a dog on it in place of where your personality used to be? This isn't you!

POPPY. You don't get to tell me who I am.

NIKKI. No, and I get it, I do, and it's my fault. I drove you to this, but you can't just... I fucked up, alright? I did. One time. When you postponed the wedding that really hurt me, and –

POPPY. I never... I just asked for a little time, because work was crazy, and –

NIKKI. But I want to fix things. I'm going to make it up to you. I'm here to save you, Poppy – save you from this sad grey Brexit-voting shithole that closes at 5 p.m. and thinks halloumi skewers constitute a thriving cultural scene.

POPPY. That isn't fair. That isn't –

NIKKI. Come home with me.

POPPY. What?

NIKKI. You know you want to.

POPPY. No.

NIKKI. Pops –

POPPY. No. Get out. I mean it.

'Coles Corner' underscore starts.

NIKKI. No you don't.

POPPY. Go! Get out! Get out! Get out!

NIKKI. Fine. You should too. While you still can.

NIKKI *goes.* POPPY *sinks to the ground. She cries. Into* –

Scene Eight

1992. JOY *is up on the balcony, looking out over the city. She's been crying. Music plays.*

Song: 'Coles Corner'

JOY. HOLD BACK THE NIGHT FROM US
    CHERISH THE LIGHT FOR US
    DON'T LET THE SHADOWS HOLD BACK THE DAWN

    COLD CITY LIGHTS GLOWING
    THE TRAFFIC OF LIFE IS FLOWING
    OUT OVER THE RIVERS AND ON INTO DARK

    I'M GOING DOWNTOWN WHERE THERE'S MUSIC
    I'M GOING WHERE VOICES FILL THE AIR
    MAYBE THERE'S SOMEONE WAITING FOR ME
    WITH A SMILE AND A FLOWER FOR MY HAIR

    I'M GOING DOWN TOWN WHERE THERE'S PEOPLE
    THE LONELINESS HANGS IN THE AIR
    WITH NO ONE THERE REAL WAITING FOR ME
    NO SMILE, NO FLOWER, NOWHERE

    COLD CITY LIGHTS GLOWING
    THE TRAFFIC OF LIFE IS FLOWING

Instrumental/movement sequence. At the end of it, GEORGE *appears next to* JOY.

GEORGE. Hey. You okay?

JOY. Does she hate me?

GEORGE. No.

JOY. Has something happened?

GEORGE. No, nothing. (*Beat.*) Our father's birthday today. She always gets –

JOY. I'm sorry.

GEORGE. Not your fault. And what's got into you?

JOY. Nothing. It's nothing, it's… He isn't really going to go. He can't. He's going to take me dancing.

GEORGE. I see.

JOY. We're going to build Jerusalem.

GEORGE. Listen – I don't have time to babysit you. You can cope if I leave you on your own, yeah?

JOY hugs GEORGE. *He smiles.*

I'll give you some space.

JOY. Thank you.

GEORGE. Just be careful. Boys like to promise you the world, and they mean it, but boys round here don't have anything to give.

GEORGE *goes. As* JOY *sings we see* GEORGE *pass* JIMMY. *They share a moment.*

JOY. I'M GOING DOWNTOWN WHERE THERE'S MUSIC
I'M GOING WHERE VOICES FILL THE AIR
MAYBE THERE'S SOMEONE WAITING FOR ME
WITH A SMILE AND A FLOWER FOR MY HAIR

I'M GOING DOWNTOWN WHERE THERE'S PEOPLE
THE LONELINESS HANGS IN THE AIR
WITH NO ONE THERE REAL WAITING FOR ME
NO SMILE, NO FLOWER NOWHERE

A quiet knock at the door. JOY *goes and lets in* JIMMY. *He's sheepish, on edge.*

You came.

JIMMY. Yeah.

JOY (*together*). I know you worry –

JIMMY (*together*). About earlier – it's not –

They stop, then start talking together again.

JOY (*together*). you worry about –

JIMMY (*together*). it's not you, I've just –

They stop again.

JOY (*together*). sorry –

JIMMY (*together*). sorry –

JIMMY. You go.

JOY. No, you.

> *They kiss.*
>
> (*Singing.*) HOLD BACK THE NIGHT.
>
> *They go.*

Scene Nine

CONNIE *appears. Underscore for 'There's a Storm A-Comin''*
starts to play.

CONNIE. So here's what it comes down to –
Twist or stick
Hole up here or make a run for it
Hunker down or head for higher ground
And I don't like the look of that sky
Those in the know can sense the end is nigh,
So time to cut your losses, if you can.

> *1979. A storm is brewing. Maybe we hear some radio news*
> *of Thatcher's election victory.* ROSE *is in the kitchen.*
> JAMES *runs in.*

JAMES. Mum! I saw lightning.

ROSE. We're safe inside.

JAMES. Where's Dad?

ROSE. Shush. Don't worry, it'll pass soon.

CONNIE. Sleep tight.
Things will look better in the morning light
Or so we hope, but in the sober dawn
We'll face the fallout of the days before.

1992. JOY *with* JIMMY *and* GEORGE.

JIMMY. You're sure?

GEORGE. She's no liar.

JIMMY (*to* JOY). But did you take a test?

JOY. I took five.

JIMMY. Okay then. Okay.

JOY. Jimmy –

He turns away.

What're we going to do?

GEORGE. You'll do what's right. He's going to do what's right.

CONNIE. And here's what it comes down to –
    Do you belong, or only passing through?
    No shame in that – no need to put down roots –
    No reason not to hit the road again.

2017. MARCUS *comforts* POPPY. *She has a drink.*

MARCUS. But where?

POPPY. I don't know. Back to my parents' for a while, God
    help me.

MARCUS. No –

POPPY. No, you're right. Terrible idea.

MARCUS. What exactly did she say to you?

POPPY. It wasn't what she said, it's just… She reminded me
    I don't belong.

CONNIE. No, I don't like the look of that sky.
    Pressure building – got to break soon.

Song: 'There's a Storm A-Comin''

VOICE 1. THERE'S A STORM A-COMIN'
    YOU'D BETTER RUN
    THERE'S A STORM A-COMIN'

GOODBYE TO THE SUN
THERE'S A STORM A-COMIN'
YOU'D BETTER RUN, BOY, RUN
YOU'D BETTER RUN

1979. HARRY *has just arrived home*. ROSE *meets him*.

ROSE. Where have you been?

HARRY. Over. It's over.

ROSE. You mean – ?

HARRY. All had our marching orders. Lucky to have lasted this long.

ROSE. Okay. Okay, well we knew... We'll find another... Just come here.

She embraces him.

Harry, you're frozen.

1992. JIMMY *and* JOY – GEORGE *has now gone*.
COMPANY *sing over the top of the scene.*

COMPANY. THERE'S A SHIP THAT'S SAILING
OUT IN THE NIGHT
THERE'S A HEART THAT'S BREAKING
I THINK IT'S MINE
THERE'S A STORM A-COMIN'
YOU'D BETTER RUN, BOY, RUN
YOU'D BETTER RUN

JIMMY. Did you...? Joy, I've got to ask. Did you want this? Did you plan – ?

JOY. How can you ask me that?

JIMMY. I could've got out. We both could've... That night – it was meant to change everything.

JOY. You don't have to stay.

2017. NIKKI *leaves Poppy a voicemail*. VIVIENNE *and* CHARLES *are doing the same*.

NIKKI. Poppy. I'm sorry, okay. Jesus.

VIVIENNE. Darling. I'm trying not to worry but you did sound a little off.

NIKKI. I tried your work. They said you were signed off. I don't… Just call me.

VIVIENNE. Please let me know that you've got this. Don't shut us out again.

Meanwhile POPPY *is making her own call.*

POPPY. Hi. Yes, thank you. Yes, on the market as soon as possible. Good.

1992. Same moment.

JIMMY. Listen. There are ways we can deal with this, aren't there, if we want to?

JOY. Deal with – ?

JIMMY. If *you* want to.

COMPANY. EVERY LITTLE PART OF YOU
    IS A MIRACLE OF MOLECULES
    BUT EVERY LITTLE THING YOU DO
    IS SO SAD, IN THE END
    OH IN THE END

Music swells. In 2017, POPPY *is alone. In 1979,* ROSE *holds a broken* HARRY*. In 1992,* JOY *and* JIMMY *face off. Around them, a riot. We hear clips from various election speeches/news bulletins: Thatcher's 1979 victory speech ('Where there is discord may we bring harmony'), Kinnock's Sheffield rally ('We're alright!'), perhaps bits of Grenfell, Brexit, etc.*

    TAKE A LAST LOOK AT THE SKY
    THROUGH THE HANGMAN'S NOOSE
    YOU'VE SHAKEN ALL THE STONES
    OF ANY FOUNDATION OF FAITH
    YOU HAD LEFT IN YOU TO LOSE
    THE HANGMAN WILL SHOW YOU A WINDOW

TO A PLACE WHERE YOU MUST GO
YOU'RE A BAD MAN TO HURT HER SO!

THERE'S A STORM A-COMIN'
YOU'D BETTER RUN
THERE'S A STORM A-COMIN'
GOODBYE TO THE SUN
THERE'S A STORM A-COMIN'
YOU'D BETTER RUN
YOU'RE A BAD MAN TO HURT HER SO

Music explodes. The storm is raging stronger than ever.
In this moment, everyone feels hugely lost and uncertain.

THERE'S A STORM A-COMIN'
THERE'S A STORM A-COMIN'
THERE'S A STORM A-COMIN' FOR YOU
YOU'D BETTER RUN, BOY, RUN, YOU'D BETTER RUN

THERE'S A STORM A-COMIN'
THERE'S A STORM A-COMIN'
THERE'S A STORM A-COMIN'
THERE'S A STORM A-COMIN'

End of Act Two.

ACT THREE

Scene One

Time has jumped forward again: HARRY *and* ROSE *are in* <u>1985</u>, JOY *and* JIMMY *in* <u>2002</u>, POPPY *in* <u>2019</u>. *The following number is delivered by the full* COMPANY, *with soloists taking the verses. It should feel percussive, a rhythmical hammering.*

Song: 'Standing at the Sky's Edge'

SOLO 1. JOSEPH WAS A GOOD MAN
   THOUGH HE KILLED HIS WIFE
   HIS HUNGRY LITTLE CHILDREN
   HE TOOK THEIR LIVES
   THIS WAS THE ACT OF A DESPERATE MAN
   WITH ONLY LOVE IN HIS EYES, NO EVIL HANDS

COMPANY. HE WAS STANDING AT THE SKY'S EDGE
   AND OUT THERE WHO KNOWS WHAT HE'S THINKING
   HE WAS SLIDING DOWN THE RAZOR'S EDGE
   AND WATCHED HIS LIFE SLOWLY SINKING
   AWAY, AWAY

SOLO 2. MARY WAS A TROUBLED GIRL
   SHE STOLE TO EAT
   SHE HAD TO SELL HER BODY
   TO PUT SHOES ON HER FEET
   STOLE A CAR AND TRIED TO GET AWAY
   NOW ALL SHE HEARS IS THE RAIN ON THE ROOF
   AT SKY'S EDGE JAIL

COMPANY. SHE WAS STANDING AT THE SKY'S EDGE
   AND OUT THERE WHO KNOWS WHAT SHE'S
     THINKING
   SHE WAS SLIDING DOWN THE RAZOR'S EDGE
   AND WATCHED HER LIFE SLOWLY SINKING
   AWAY, AWAY

CONNIE. So this is where you find us
    Clinging on by our fingertips
    Almost out of gas on a long stretch of highway
    Just trying to eke out another mile
    But it's falling apart, this hunk of junk,
    It's not the thing you were promised –
    Jerusalem fading in your rear-view mirror
    And knowing you were sold a lie.
    But the kids in the back are still sleeping
    So there's nothing to do but drive.

COMPANY. THEY WERE STANDING AT THE SKY'S EDGE
    AND OUT THERE WHO KNOWS WHAT THEY'RE
        THINKING
    THEY WERE SLIDING DOWN THE RAZOR'S EDGE
    AND WATCHED THEIR LIVES SLOWLY SINKING
    AWAY, AWAY, AWAY, AWAY, AWAY

SOLO 3. JACOB WAS MISGUIDED, HE CARRIED A BLADE
    SO MUCH FEAR IN THE CITY IT CARRIED HIM AWAY
    YOUNG MEN WERE FIGHTING
    AND LOSING THEIR LIVES
    AT NIGHT AS THE SCREECH OWLS IN THE TREES
    WATCH YOUNG MEN DIE

COMPANY. THEY WERE STANDING AT THE SKY'S EDGE
    AND OUT THERE WHO KNOWS WHAT THEY'RE
        THINKING
    THEY WERE SLIDING DOWN THE RAZOR'S EDGE
    AND WATCHED THEIR LIVES SLOWLY SINKING

    THEY WERE STANDING AT THE SKY'S EDGE
    AND OUT THERE THERE'S DANGEROUS THINKING
    THEY WERE SLIDING DOWN THE MIRROR'S EDGE
    AND WATCHED THEIR LIVES SLOWLY SINKING
    AWAY, AWAY, AWAY, AWAY, AWAY, AWAY

Scene Two

<u>1985</u>. HARRY is home with TREV, *a former work friend, and Trev's son* NIGEL. HARRY *is dishevelled and withdrawn.*

TREV. Anyway, there's nowt doing, I'm afraid.

HARRY. Sorry, what is…?

TREV. Safeway. Your Rose was asking, and I thought there might've been summat in the warehouse, but –

HARRY. Right.

TREV. Nowt you would've wanted anyway.

HARRY. She shouldn't have asked you.

TREV. No shame in asking.

HARRY. State of… Youngest foreman in history, you know that? And now…

TREV. We're all going through it.

HARRY. Aye. Should be grateful for owt I can get.

TREV. Didn't mean it like that.

HARRY. True though. (*Beat.*) You know that was it – the overwhelming emotion when we first moved in here – gratitude. Not joy, or excitement, or… or trepidation. Just gratitude. Relief. Back before the lifts broke and the ceilings leaked and the rats got in the walls. Way back when. Cos we'd come from slums, near enough, and this were paradise, and we were so grateful that we never stopped, never saw the con, never thought to question why we were in the slum to begin with – why some other bastard had to be the one to lift us up. Cos it blinds you, that gratitude, teaches us to be humble, to doff our caps and thank our lucky stars for whatever crumbs we can catch. (*Beat. To* NIGEL.) And you go back Tuesday?

NIGEL. Aye.

HARRY. Suppose we should be grateful for that too.

NIGEL. Not how we wanted it, but –

HARRY. No.

TREV. But you can be proud.

HARRY. No, you can – of course you can.

TREV. You walk back in wi' your head held high.

HARRY. I didn't mean –

NIGEL. S'alright.

HARRY. I'd never… No. It's a real thing you've done, however it's ended, and a bastard thing that were done to you. We'll all be there at the gates – steel stands with the miners.

NIGEL. You don't have to.

HARRY. Cos it weren't just for you, it were for all of us. So I am, I am grateful for… You don't strike because you want to. No one wants to. You strike to say 'I'm still here. I still matter. You will see me.' That's where we went wrong. No one sees us up here – that's why we're left to rot. Stand up. Go on – stand up, let me look at you.

NIGEL is a bit thrown by this, but gets to his feet. HARRY grips him by the shoulders. It's uncomfortable.

I see you. Do you hear me? I see you. You are seen.

TREV. Alright, take it easy.

HARRY. Sorry. Sorry. Don't know what…

TREV. No bother. Daft lad.

HARRY. Yeah. (*Beat.*) Well, don't let me keep you.

At this point, ROSE enters. She's dressed smartly, just returned from work.

ROSE. Afternoon, gents. Trev! It's good to see you.

TREV. And you.

ROSE. And it can't be – is this little Nigel?

NIGEL. Alright, Mrs Stanhope.

ROSE. Look at the size of you! Don't know where the time's
gone. And it's wedding bells this summer, that right?

NIGEL. It is, yeah – August. Won't be owt fancy, but –

ROSE. Well, I wish you a lifetime of happiness.

HARRY. They were just on their way out.

ROSE. You sure? I could stick a pot on. Don't suppose you've
had much hospitality from His Majesty.

TREV. Nah, you're alright. Should be making tracks.

ROSE. Alright, well, don't be strangers. And we'll be there to
see you back on Tuesday – all the women will.

TREV. Take care now. Good to see you, Harry.

   HARRY *doesn't respond, already withdrawn.* ROSE *sees out*
   TREV *and* NIGEL.

ROSE. Good of them to drop by. (*Beat.*) Harry? Said it were
nice –

HARRY. You embarrassed me.

ROSE. What's that?

HARRY. We don't beg.

ROSE. What're you talking about?

HARRY. Safeway.

ROSE. Oh. (*Beat.*) If it's an apology you're wanting, you'll be
waiting a while.

HARRY. I've told you over and –

ROSE. So change the record. Cos I've been on my feet all day
and I don't want to hear it. I've got tea to get on, and laundry,
and I won't – I will not stand here and be snapped at for trying
to find you something to fill your days. I haven't given up on
you, even if you have. (*Beat.*) I'll put the kettle on.

*ROSE turns away from HARRY. A shift. Music plays.
NIGEL reappears and sings.*

Song: 'Our Darkness'

NIGEL. WHEN EVENING SHADOWS FADE
    I TURN TO MY TRUE LOVE
    SHE HAS THE STRENGTH TO SAY
    THE WORDS THAT I CANNOT

    IN DARKNESS, OUR DARKNESS
    SO HEARTLESS, THIS DARKNESS

    I'M LOST HERE IN THE GREY
    I WAIT FOR YOUR RETURNING
    I WATCH THE FIRELIGHT PLAY
    FLAMES FLICKER WITH MY YEARNING

    FOR DARKNESS, OUR DARKNESS
    SO HEARTFELT, THIS DARKNESS

*The WOMEN of the company emerge holding carnations.
They're led by CATHY, Nigel's fiancée.*

CATHY. THROUGH STREETS AND AVENUES
    WILL YOU COME BACK TO YOUR LOVER?
    THE PLACE FOR ME AND YOU
    IS HERE WITH NO OTHER

*A line of MINERS appear and start to slowly cross the stage,
returning to work.*

NIGEL/CATHY. IN DARKNESS, OUR DARKNESS
    SO HEARTFELT, THIS DARKNESS

*The WOMEN line up to give carnations to the MINERS. It's
solemn, tender and dignified.*

COMPANY. MY ARMS THEY OPEN UP FOR YOU
    AND WHERE THEY FALL IT CUTS THE ROOT
    WE TALK OF UNDERSTANDING
    AND WE TALK OF LOVE

*By the end of this, the MINERS and the WOMEN are gone,
leaving only HARRY and ROSE.*

HARRY/ROSE. WHEN EVENING SHADOWS CHANGE
   I TURN BACK TO MY TRUE LOVE
   SHE HAS THE STRENGTH TO SAY
   THE WORDS THAT I CANNOT
   IN DARKNESS, OUR DARKNESS
   SO HEARTFELT, OUR DARKNESS
   SO HEARTLESS, THIS DARKNESS
   OUR DARKNESS, IN DARKNESS

   WE TALK OF LOVE

Song ends.

Scene Three

2019. POPPY *with* VIVIENNE.

VIVIENNE. The whole office?

POPPY. Yeah. Apparently, they'd been haemorrhaging money
   for months. They thought they were getting this huge new
   pharmaceutical client, but they ended up going with
   somewhere in Frankfurt, and that was the final straw.

VIVIENNE. Right.

POPPY. Should've seen it coming, really. Anyway, anyway, I was
   talking to Marcus, about how much I was loving the freelance
   life, and he said he might do the same, so we could work on
   some projects together.

VIVIENNE. But still staying up here?

POPPY. He knows the local scene better than anyone.

VIVIENNE. Right. But you don't actually *need* to be here, do
   you? Not as a freelancer?

POPPY. What do you mean?

VIVIENNE. Only that – and don't bite my head off for saying
   it – but surely there must be more opportunities in London?

POPPY. I know the market here.

VIVIENNE. And you did say you were moving back. When you had your little wobble. You did tell us –

POPPY. I worked through that.

VIVIENNE. I know.

POPPY. I'm fine now. And what's in London that isn't here? The job market's screwed everywhere. Housing is ridiculous. There isn't any –

VIVIENNE. Just so long as you're happy.

POPPY. I am. Why wouldn't I be?

VIVIENNE. Good. Then I'm glad. I'm proud of you – we both are – after everything you've… Maybe I'll do the same. Maybe I'll leave your father and find myself a little hermitage in the Shetlands and start everything over.

POPPY. That's nothing like what I've done.

VIVIENNE. I wasn't –

POPPY. Half a million people live here. This is the fourth largest city in the country. People are always surprised when they hear that. It's not –

VIVIENNE. Okay, okay! Well, maybe I'll buy one of the new flats on the wing they've just finished then.

POPPY. What?

VIVIENNE. Didn't you say they were about to go on sale?

POPPY (*noncommittal*). Mmm.

VIVIENNE. Wouldn't you love to have your old mother as your neighbour?

POPPY. Mum – is everything okay? Between you and Dad?

VIVIENNE. Yes, yes, of course. Being silly. Nothing to report.

POPPY. You're sure?

VIVIENNE. I'm sure. He's very excited to have you for Christmas. He's ordered a goose, which he seems very invested in.

POPPY. Great.

VIVIENNE. It'll be nice to have you home, anyway.

Scene ends.

Scene Four

Into 2002. JOY enters with GRACE and CONSTANCE, Joy's ten-year-old daughter. They're all bundled up from the cold. In the distance, Christmas music plays.

JOY. Come on, superstar – it's freezing.

CONSTANCE. But I wanted to be Mary.

GRACE. I think you'll make a wonderful Wise Man.

CONSTANCE. The beard's all itchy.

JOY. We'll work something out. (*To* GRACE.) Will you stay for tea? We're having fish fingers.

GRACE. I don't think so – I'd rather leave while it's light.

CONSTANCE. Do you miss living here, Auntie Grace?

GRACE. I'm very happy where I am now.

CONSTANCE. Nana Rose doesn't like to visit us either.

JOY. That isn't... And we'll be seeing her on Christmas Eve.

CONSTANCE (*to* GRACE). Do you want a Christmas chocolate before you go? We're only allowed one a day. (*Calling off.*) Dad! Daddy! I'm going to eat your chocolate.

GRACE. I should be going.

JOY. Say hello, at least. Please?

> JIMMY *emerges. He looks older, tired. He wears a security guard's uniform.*

JIMMY. There you are. Thought I heard a herd of elephants in the kitchen.

CONSTANCE. Just us.

JIMMY. How are you, Grace?

GRACE (*curtly*). Well, thank you. I'll see you all soon. (*To* CONSTANCE.) Practise being wise. Be good now.

> GRACE *goes.*

JOY (*to* JIMMY). Sorry. How are you? Did you sleep?

JIMMY. Yeah, a bit. You just caught me – I'm off in ten.

JOY. Like ships in the night.

CONSTANCE. Will you help me with my lines?

JOY. Of course. Go on – I'll be through in a minute.

> CONSTANCE *goes another way to her bedroom.*

JIMMY. I'm on till four. I'll try not to wake you coming in.

JOY. Don't worry. I don't mind it. I like knowing you're there.

JIMMY. That's not what you say at four in the morning.

JOY. We'll get this all sorted soon. You won't be on nights forever, I'll be fully qualified, we'll work out a, a… (*She yawns.*) Sorry.

JIMMY. It's okay.

JOY. I hate this. I live with you and I still miss you.

JIMMY. Only way to stop you getting sick of me.

JOY. The older nurses all say the first year's the hardest. It gets easier.

JIMMY. You're doing great. Oh, and a bit of good news – Christmas Eve's covered. I'll be working overnight on New Year's though.

JOY. That's okay – I'm starting early anyway.

JIMMY. Yeah?

JOY. Five, I think. (*Beat.*) It won't be forever. I was talking to Stacey – she says they'll be starting the renovations next year.

JIMMY. Heard that before.

JOY. They'll have to – now it's listed they can't do anything else with it.

JIMMY. We could put in for rehousing – fresh start –

JOY. No –

JIMMY. Everyone's doing it. Emptying out, like rats on a sinking… Rats are the only buggers who've stayed.

JOY. It will get better – the city *has* got better –

JIMMY. Not this far up the hill.

JOY. It's not like when I first came.

JIMMY. I just… We should think about it. I don't want to die here.

JOY. I don't want you to die anywhere.

JIMMY. I'm serious.

JOY. So where would you go? Still got your sights set on Mars?

JIMMY. No! Just… a proper fresh start. Clean slate. (*Beat.*) Australia.

JOY. Australia?

JIMMY. Why not? I know a couple of lads who did. You can nurse anywhere – I'd find something. This time next year, Christmas on the beach.

JOY. And what about Constance?

JIMMY. She'd love it.

JOY. No.

JIMMY. Just no?

JOY. She finishes school here – nothing disrupts… I won't let what happened to me happen to her.

Beat.

JIMMY. Right.

JOY. I didn't mean… I had plans for me, plans for us, and I have plans for her now. Everything we need is here. (*She kisses him.*) I love you.

JIMMY. I know. Don't wait up.

JIMMY *steps out of the flat and* JOY *goes. As* JIMMY *sings this number he's joined by others – packing up, preparing for journeys, moving on.*

Song: 'Midnight Train'

I KNOW IT'S TIME TO TRAVEL
IT'S THE THING THAT TAKES A LIFE
IF I REMEMBER KNOWING WHO I AM
MAYBE IT'LL BE ALRIGHT
BUT I'VE GOT TO LEAVE IT HERE
I'VE GOT TO LEAVE YOU HERE

I KNOW I GAVE NO REASONS
AND NOTHING HERE IS CLEAR
BUT WHAT IT IS I'M FEELING
OH, IT'S GIVING ME THE FEAR
I'VE GOT TO GET AWAY
I'VE GOT TO GET AWAY

IT'S TIME THAT I WAS LEAVING
AS THOSE SHADOWS FALL
ON THE MIDNIGHT TRAIN

IN TIME YOU KNOW I'D LEAVE YOU RUNNING
I JUST DON'T FIT THE WORLD
THIS IS SOMETHING THAT I'VE TRIED
BUT IT JUST DON'T WORK
IS THERE SOME OTHER WAY?
OH, IS THERE ANOTHER WAY?

COMPANY. OH, IS THERE ANOTHER WAY?

JIMMY. I CAN'T EXPLAIN OR REASON
   I JUST DON'T FEEL ALRIGHT
   I KNOW I'VE TRIED TO SMILE AND WAVE
   BUT I'VE GOT NO FIGHT
   LEFT IN ME, BABE
   NO NOT IN ME, BABE

   IT'S TIME THAT I WAS LEAVING
   AS THOSE SHADOWS FALL
   ON THE MIDNIGHT TRAIN
   THE MIDNIGHT TRAIN

   AND EVEN AS WE ROLL AWAY
   THE WEIGHT BEGINS TO FALL
   I DIDN'T LEAVE A NOTE FOR YOU
   I JUST HURRIED DOWN THE HALL
   THERE'S NO OTHER WAY
   THERE'S NO OTHER WAY

   IT'S TIME THAT I WAS LEAVING
   AS THOSE SHADOWS FALL
   ON THE MIDNIGHT TRAIN
   IT'S TIME THAT I WAS LEAVING
   AS THAT WHISTLE BLOWS
   FOR THE MIDNIGHT TRAIN
   MIDNIGHT TRAIN
   THE MIDNIGHT TRAIN
   ON THE MIDNIGHT TRAIN

Scene Five

1985. By the time the song ends, ROSE *and* HARRY *are onstage.* ROSE *has a large, packed suitcase with her,* HARRY *slouched in his armchair.* ROSE *is on the verge of tears, but is trying to be resolute.*

HARRY. Right.

ROSE. Couldn't bring myself to before Christmas, but I can't start another New Year like this.

HARRY. I see.

ROSE. Do you?

HARRY. Not much I can offer you right now.

ROSE. It isn't about that. It was never about that.

HARRY. You got some fancy man waiting?

ROSE. Harry –

HARRY. Wouldn't blame you. Not a soul in the world got use for a man like me.

ROSE. So that's it, is it?

HARRY. What else do you want?

ROSE. Right. Don't get up then.

HARRY. What do you want from me?

ROSE. I want you to fight! And I know, I know, you never got owt without fighting, it's all you've ever done, but for me – for *us* – fight to... I can't do it, Harry. I can't keep carrying us both. And I've never asked you for anything but I am asking now. Fight for me. Don't end up like... Because walking out this door is the hardest thing I'll ever do, and the only way – the *only way* I come back is if you come and carry me back through it.

HARRY. Is that right, Mrs Stanhope?

ROSE. I reckon. (*Beat.*) I'll be at my mother's. James is there already.

HARRY. Right.

ROSE. There's leftovers in the fridge, and a week's worth of meals in the freezer.

No response.

Don't leave it too long now, eh?

She goes. A pause. Music starts. HARRY stands.

HARRY. Rose –

He loses his nerve and sits again. Music starts. As HARRY sings, he watches a silent version of his parents moving through the flat before him, growing ever further apart.

Song: 'For Your Lover Give Some Time'

IT WAS YOUR BIRTHDAY YESTERDAY
I GAVE A GIFT
THAT ALMOST TOOK YOUR BREATH AWAY
BUT TO BE HONEST
I NEARLY LEFT IT ON THE TRAIN
FOR YOUR LOVER GIVE SOME TIME

YOU TALK FOREVER ON THE PHONE
TO YOUR MOTHER
AND WITH MY THOUGHTS I'M LEFT ALONE
NOW AND THEN
I THINK HOW STRANGE OUR LOVE HAS GROWN
FOR YOUR LOVER GIVE SOME TIME

I WILL GIVE UP THESE CIGARETTES
STAY AT HOME AND WATCH YOU
MEND THE TEARS IN YOUR DRESS
HAVE YOUR NAME IN A ROSE
TATTOOED ACROSS MY CHEST
AND BE YOUR LOVER FOR ALL TIME

MAYBE I WILL DRINK A LITTLE LESS
COME HOME EARLY
AND NOT COMPLAIN ABOUT THE DEBTS
AND GIVE YOU FLOWERS

FROM THE GRAVEYARD NOW AND THEN
FOR YOUR LOVER GIVE SOME TIME

I THINK OF PLACES THAT I'VE SEEN
A SKIPPING STONE
ACROSS THE OCEAN I HAVE BEEN
A ROOTLESS SOUL
WITH NO ONE ELSE TO SHARE MY DREAMS
AND FOR MY LOVER GAVE NO TIME

SO I'LL TOAST TO YOU AGAIN
TO ALL THE CINEMAS
WE RAN IN FROM THE RAIN
LAUGHING, CLUTCHING
SOAKING NEWSPAPERS TO YOUR FACE
AND FOR YOUR LOVE YOU GAVE SOME TIME

I WILL GIVE UP THESE CIGARETTES
STAY AT HOME AND WATCH YOU
MEND THE TEARS IN YOUR DRESS
HAVE YOUR NAME IN A ROSE
TATTOOED ACROSS MY CHEST
AND BE YOUR LOVER FOR ALL TIME

MAYBE I WILL DRINK A LITTLE LESS
COME HOME EARLY
AND NOT COMPLAIN ABOUT THE DEBTS
AND GIVE YOU FLOWERS
FROM THE GRAVEYARD NOW AND THEN
FOR YOUR LOVER GIVE SOME TIME
FOR YOUR LOVER GIVE SOME TIME

In 2002, a phone rings. JOY, *bleary-eyed, in her dressing gown, answers it.* JIMMY, *at work, appears with an old 2000s mobile.*

JOY. Hello?

JIMMY. Hey. It's me.

JOY. What's…? Are you okay? Has something happened?

JIMMY. No, I'm fine. Were you sleeping?

JOY. Of course I was sleeping.

JIMMY. Right. Sorry.

JOY. What's the matter?

JIMMY. Nothing, just… They're letting me off early. Should make it back to ring in the New Year after all.

JOY (*stifling a yawn*). Oh.

JIMMY. But you'd rather be asleep, wouldn't you?

JOY. Sorry – it's just I've got to be up so early.

JIMMY. Yeah – no, this was stupid – I'm stupid.

JOY. No, it's okay. (*Beat.*) Can I go back to bed now please?

JIMMY. Yeah, course. (*Remembers.*) Oh – there was just one other thing.

JOY. Right?

JIMMY. I don't want to move to Australia.

JOY. Oh. (*Beat.*) Good?

JIMMY. I mean unless you want to. Do you want to?

JOY. No.

JIMMY. No. Course. Good. I just want to be wherever you are, and anywhere you are, that's fine by me – that's home. And I know – I know you had a plan and this wasn't it and we're mostly just knackered all the time, but I wouldn't change a thing – not one thing about any of it. I love you.

JOY. I love you too. (*Yawns.*)

JIMMY. Sorry. It felt really important, really urgent to tell you all that right this second, but I'm actually just being dead selfish, aren't I?

JOY. Don't be daft. You can always call to say you love me.

JIMMY. I'll try not to wake you when I get in.

JOY. No – do. I want to see in the New Year with you.

JIMMY. Okay.

Moment ends, and they go. In 2019, POPPY appears in the flat. Others go.

POPPY. I THINK OF PLACES THAT I'VE SEEN
    A SKIPPING STONE
    ACROSS THE OCEAN I HAVE BEEN
    A ROOTLESS SOUL
    WITH NO ONE ELSE TO SHARE MY DREAMS
    AND FOR MY LOVER GAVE NO TIME

NIKKI appears up on the balcony. She holds a bottle of fizz and is wrapped up from the cold. She sings.

NIKKI. SO I'LL TOAST TO YOU AGAIN
    TO ALL THE CINEMAS
    WE RAN IN FROM THE RAIN
    LAUGHING, CLUTCHING
    SOAKING NEWSPAPERS TO YOUR FACE
    AND FOR YOUR LOVE YOU GAVE SOME TIME

They harmonise together.

NIKKI/POPPY. I WILL GIVE UP THESE CIGARETTES
    STAY AT HOME AND WATCH YOU
    MEND THE TEARS IN YOUR DRESS
    HAVE YOUR NAME IN A ROSE
    TATTOOED ACROSS MY CHEST
    AND BE YOUR LOVER FOR ALL TIME

    MAYBE I WILL DRINK A LITTLE LESS
    COME HOME EARLY
    AND NOT COMPLAIN ABOUT THE DEBTS
    AND GIVE YOU FLOWERS
    FROM THE GRAVEYARD NOW AND THEN
    AND FOR MY LOVER GIVE SOME TIME
    FOR YOUR LOVER GIVE SOME TIME

Scene Six

2019. POPPY *is having a New Year's Eve party. With her are* MARCUS, *his boyfriend* MAX, CONNIE, SEB, ALICE, KAREN, JUSTINE *and* JENNY (*other party guests*).

MAX. Hold on – is this the cat lady or the neck tattoo?

POPPY. It was a face tattoo.

MARCUS. Is that better or worse?

POPPY. Shut up. And it doesn't matter, because I'm not going to ask either of them out anyway.

MAX (*to others*). Next year is all about getting Poppy laid.

POPPY. Nobody encourage him.

MARCUS. Has she told you about my first visit here? Doesn't know anyone – invites me over for a bit of aubergine –

POPPY. Stop it!

MARCUS. Busts out the Ottolenghi, plies me with booze, and I'm thinking 'God, she does know I'm gay, right?' Then reckons *I* was hitting on *her.*

POPPY. He bought me condiments – what's a girl to think?

MARCUS. So there we are, two narcissistic queers, each wondering how we're going to let the other one down.

JUSTINE (*to* POPPY). So what're you doing? Are you online, or – ?

KAREN. I do Guardian Soulmates.

ALICE. Stay single while you can – enjoy it. He loves Sheffield Wednesday more than he loves me.

SEB. I love Sheffield United more than I love you.

POPPY. Shall we talk about something else? Who needs a drink?

MAX. Nope. Poppy – how long have you lived here now?

POPPY. A little over four years. Why?

MAX. And how many dates have you been on in that time?

POPPY. This is bullying. You're all bullies.

CONNIE. Not actually zero, though? Seriously?

JENNY. Jesus. I'd be worried I'd have forgotten how.

MARCUS. That's what I said!

POPPY. It isn't easy! What if there's just no one here for me?

KAREN. Come on, Yorkshire's dripping with lesbians – we've got Hebden Bridge.

JUSTINE. Ooh! You know Amy's sister is single again – they might be out tonight.

JENNY. I'll text her.

POPPY. Don't! I don't need… Can you all just drink and shut up, please?

ALICE. Such a hostess.

A doorbell rings.

MAX. Strippers are here.

POPPY. One sec.

POPPY *starts to head to the door.*

MAX (*to* JENNY). Make sure you tell her she's available and desperate.

POPPY (*over her shoulder*). Ugh, you are such a nightmare.

JUSTINE. You'll thank us later.

POPPY *opens the door. A shift in light.* NIKKI *is there.* POPPY *freezes.*

NIKKI. Happy New Year.

POPPY. Oh Christ.

NIKKI. Can I come in? (*Beat.*) Pops? Freezing out here.

MARCUS. Who is it?

ALICE. You're letting a draught in!

NIKKI. Got company?

SEB. Oi, Poppy! Put wood in't hole!

POPPY (*with resignation*). Fuck it. Why not?

> POPPY *allows* NIKKI *in. The group can sense something is wrong.*

NIKKI. Oh, right. Hi. Hello. (*To* POPPY.) Thought you might be…

POPPY. What? (*Beat.*) Oh. Alone.

NIKKI. I'm stupid. Sorry.

MARCUS (*to* POPPY). Wait – is this who I think it is?

NIKKI (*attempting jocularity*). Oh, that doesn't sound good.

POPPY. This is Nikki, yeah.

MARCUS. Fuck.

NIKKI. Okay, that's really not good.

MAX. Um, what do you think you're doing here?

NIKKI. Uh, I don't think that's any of your business.

MARCUS. I think maybe you should leave.

POPPY. It's fine.

NIKKI (*to* MARCUS). Alright, Sean Bean, it's fine. Stand down.

POPPY. Jesus. Okay, we're doing this. Uh. This is Max, his partner Marcus, Karen, Alice and Seb, Jenny and Justine, Connie.

NIKKI. Hi.

POPPY. This is the woman who ruined my life, so –

NIKKI. Maybe we could talk in private for a minute?

POPPY. I'm having a party.

NIKKI. Right.

CONNIE (*to* POPPY). Do you want us to go?

POPPY. No, it's fine.

NIKKI (*to* CONNIE). Hold on – do I know you?

CONNIE. Uh…

NIKKI. You showed me a flat.

CONNIE. Oh. I might've done.

NIKKI. And now you're…? (*To* POPPY.) Did you invite your estate agent to your New Year's Eve party?

POPPY. It's not –

NIKKI. Because that is… Or do you just fancy her? (*To* CONNIE.) You might think you're too young, but she does have a type.

POPPY. What do you want, Nikki?

NIKKI. She is very pretty. (*To* CONNIE.) You are very pretty, but you lied to me.

CONNIE. Excuse me?

NIKKI. You did. They did kick people out. They promised them they could come back, but as soon as they'd finished tarting them up they flogged them all off to posh pricks like her.

POPPY. I'm sorry – are you here to win me back or tell me off?

NIKKI. I don't know. Both, maybe. (*To others*.) Hi everyone. Sorry for… So I'm Nikki. The ex-fiancée. Did you know I had to propose three times before she actually believed I meant it? But then Poppy has always had trouble taking me seriously.

POPPY. What are you trying to do?

NIKKI (*still to others*). Anyway, I did finally convince her – New Year's Eve, it was – what – five years ago? So it's our anniversary, sort of. Cheers. But then she calls off the wedding, and I do something awful, and then poof! She's vanished. Fresh start. Scorched earth. And I don't think that's fair.

POPPY. You want to talk about what's fair?

NIKKI. You know what I had to do, after you left? I had to move in with my brother and his wife and their fucking two-year-old twins. I had to sell eighty per cent of everything I owned and live out of two suitcases. I couldn't just start over. I couldn't waltz into a new life. I couldn't buy a fucking duplex in a listed building with its own Wikipedia page –

POPPY. That must've been very hard for you.

NIKKI. Yeah, it was. Actually it was.

POPPY. Good.

NIKKI. You shouldn't be here! Why do you get to be here? Why should you have all this? It was built for real people, working people, people who had nothing. Not you. Do you know whose home you're living in?

CONNIE. Mine.

Beat.

NIKKI. Sorry?

POPPY. Oh – Connie grew up on the estate.

CONNIE. Right here, actually – this flat.

POPPY. What? Really? *Here*-here?

CONNIE. Yeah. Wasn't going to tell you that. Thought you might think it was weird.

POPPY. Wow. Okay.

CONNIE (*addressing* NIKKI). I was born here, Dad was too, and his parents were some of the first in. Mum, she left everything to come here, and yeah, it saved her.

NIKKI. Right. Right then – exactly. This is what I'm saying. (*To* POPPY.) It's not for you. You've taken this woman's home –

CONNIE. Has she heck?

NIKKI. You've colonised –

CONNIE. Er, no – she bought it. Fair play to her.

NIKKI. But your family –

CONNIE. Moved on. We moved on – that's what healthy people do. You should see where I am now. I've got a garden. I've got a dog. I've got sash windows. This place – sod it, I'm off-duty – this place in't anything special. Polish some concrete and get it on *Doctor Who* and you lot think it's Nirvana. No. A home is a series of boxes that stops the rain coming in – if you're lucky. Everything else is what you put in it.

NIKKI. But –

CONNIE. And no one cared about this place until the posh pricks came along, but now they do. Now people don't shoot up in the lifts or get stabbed in the hallways and that is progress – I'll take that as a win.

POPPY. You really used to live right here?

CONNIE. I did.

POPPY. Is that why you agreed to come to my party?

CONNIE. It is a bit, yeah.

POPPY. Great.

CONNIE. Sorry.

NIKKI. I'm sorry too.

POPPY. Of course you are.

CONNIE. It's almost midnight – we should head up to the top floor for the fireworks – best view in the city.

POPPY. Yeah. Go ahead.

JENNY. Are you okay?

POPPY. Yeah, I'm fine – you go on. There's mulled wine! Keep yourselves warm.

MARCUS (*to* NIKKI). And maybe it's time for you to go now.

NIKKI. She said I could stay, so I'm staying.

Music starts.

POPPY. I never actually said that.

MAX. Do you want one of us to – ?

POPPY. No, it's all fine, honestly. I'll catch you up.

The others start to file out. In 2002, JOY enters the flat in her dressing gown, lingering by the kitchen. In 1985, HARRY also enters and slumps in his chair.

Song: 'There's a Storm A-Comin'' (Reprise)

JOY. THERE'S A STORM A-COMIN'
    YOU'D BETTER RUN
    THERE'S A STORM A-COMIN'
    GOODBYE TO THE SUN
    THERE'S A STORM A-COMIN'
    YOU'D BETTER RUN, BOY, RUN
    YOU'D BETTER RUN

Back to Poppy's flat in 2019. Music continues under scene, brooding, building.

POPPY. Where are you staying tonight? (*Beat.*) You don't have anywhere, do you? Course you don't.

NIKKI. No.

POPPY. And I suppose now that's my problem?

NIKKI. Was counting on a holiday miracle.

    POPPY *laughs without mirth.*

    I am sorry. That wasn't what I came here to say.

POPPY. Right.

NIKKI. Pops –

POPPY. But you couldn't help yourself, could you? And actually, actually you know there's a difference between speaking truth to power and just being a twat.

NIKKI. I know.

POPPY. No, I don't think you do. I am not responsible for…
It's a shitty old world, Nikki, but I'm doing my best. I have
a job I do well and neighbours I'm kind to and a series of
boxes that keep the rain out, and I'm proud of that. It wasn't
easy. I have no intention of leaving here.

NIKKI. Okay.

POPPY. Okay.

JOY. THERE'S A SHIP THAT'S SAILING

*In 1985, ROSE enters. She sees HARRY slumped in his
chair.*

ROSE. Harry?

JOY. OUT IN THE NIGHT

ROSE. You up then?

JOY. THERE'S A HEART THAT'S BREAKING

ROSE. I tried waiting, I did, but…

JOY. I THINK IT'S MINE

ROSE. It's New Year.

JOY. THERE'S A STORM A-COMIN'

ROSE. Fine. Don't get up.

JOY. YOU'D BETTER RUN, BOY, RUN
YOU'D BETTER RUN

2019.

POPPY. I need to join my friends.

NIKKI. So I should go?

POPPY. You can do what you like.

NIKKI. Right. (*Beat.*) Only thing is, it's eleven fifty-nine. On
New Year's Eve.

POPPY. So what?

NIKKI. So just look at me, Poppy. Pops – look at me – please.

1985.

ROSE. Just let me talk to you. Or talk to me. Please.

2019.

NIKKI. I've done this all so badly.

1985.

ROSE. Will you listen for once, you daft bugger?

Music shifts. In 2019, up on the bridge, Poppy's GUESTS *are counting in the New Year.*

GUESTS. Ten!

2002. JIMMY *is on his way home. A* TEENAGER *emerges from the shadows.*

TEEN. Mate – here, mate – come here a sec.

2019.

GUESTS. Nine!

1985.

ROSE. Harry?

2019. In the flat.

NIKKI. Look at me.

GUESTS. Eight!

2002.

TEEN. You carrying? What you got?

JIMMY. Not me, pal.

2019.

GUESTS. Seven!

1985.

ROSE. Harry? (*Panic growing.*) No, no –

2019.

NIKKI   Poppy. Please.

GUESTS. Six!

1985.

ROSE (*calling off*). Somebody – I need... I need an ambulance.

2019.

GUESTS. Five!

1985.

ROSE. It's okay, Harry, it'll be okay.

2019.

GUESTS. Four!

2002.

TEEN. Nah. Nah, you're carrying. Show me –

JIMMY *attempts to push past the* TEEN. *A brief struggle. The* TEEN *pulls out a knife.*

2019.

NIKKI. Poppy!

GUESTS. THREE! TWO! ONE!

JIMMY *is stabbed and falls to the floor.*

1985.

ROSE. Harry!

2019.

GUESTS. Happy New Year!

We hear a clock strike twelve. Fireworks. In 1985, ROSE is desperately trying to resuscitate HARRY. In 2002, the TEEN runs off. In 2019, NIKKI looks to POPPY hopefully. POPPY holds her gaze. On the final bong, the dates crunch over into –

ACT FOUR

Scene One

The years click over. 1985 into 1986, 2002 into 2003, 2019 into 2020. Stage clears, just leaving ROSE.

Song: 'After the Rain'

ROSE. AFTER THE RAINS HAVE GONE
   SOMETHING INSIDE ME
   I KNOW IS DYING FOR YOU
   THE SLEET AND THE SNOW
   JUST DRIFT ME I KNOW AWAY

   AFTER THE RAINS HAVE GONE
   SOMETHING INSIDE ME CRIES
   WHAT'S BEHIND THAT DOOR
   THIS GIRL JUST CAN'T TAKE IT ANY MORE
   THIS GIRL JUST CAN'T TAKE IT ANY MORE

   AFTER THE PAIN HAS GONE
   I FINALLY OPEN MY EYES
   NOT CRYING ANY MORE
   WE DRIFTED APART
   IT'S BROKEN OUR HEARTS SURVIVING

   AFTER THE RAINS HAVE GONE
   SOMETHING INSIDE ME CRIES
   WHAT'S BEHIND THAT DOOR?
   THIS GIRL JUST CAN'T TAKE IT ANY MORE
   THIS GIRL JUST CAN'T TAKE IT…

The COMPANY *gradually emerge from behind her, building harmonies.*

   AFTER THE RAINS HAVE GONE
   SOMETHING INSIDE ME CRIES
   WHAT'S BEHIND THAT DOOR?

THIS GIRL JUST CAN'T TAKE IT ANY MORE
THIS GIRL JUST CAN'T TAKE IT ANY MORE

OH, I JUST CAN'T TAKE
GOT MY LOVE, DON'T WANT TO FAKE
THIS GIRL JUST CAN'T TAKE IT ANY MORE
THIS GIRL JUST CAN'T TAKE IT ANY MORE
THIS GIRL JUST CAN'T TAKE IT ANY MORE

Song ends.

1986 clicks forward to 1989. JIMMY *arrives and joins* ROSE. *He carries a cardboard box.*

JIMMY. My room's clear.

ROSE. Good lad.

JIMMY. Looks smaller.

ROSE. Not just your room – the whole estate's shrinking.

JIMMY. Tonne of mould behind the bed.

ROSE. Right.

JIMMY. Gross.

ROSE. We'll give it a scrub.

JIMMY. Who do you reckon'll get this place, once we've gone?

ROSE. Could be anyone these days.

JIMMY. Don't say it like that.

ROSE. Some of the people you see… When we moved in here – you wouldn't believe it. Streets in the sky.

JIMMY. I know.

ROSE. This place really was something once.

JIMMY. Anything I can do in here? I thought… If you wanted I could go through some of Dad's stuff. I thought maybe you wouldn't want to, so I could…

ROSE. Come here.

She hugs him.

It's all done. All sorted. You're a good boy.

JIMMY. Dean and Mike and Ricky are coming to give us a
hand with the boxes.

ROSE. You didn't have to. I was going to ask some of your
father's friends.

JIMMY. It's no bother. They owe me anyway.

ROSE. Okay.

JIMMY. And Dean proper fancies you, so –

ROSE. James!

JIMMY. Few of them do, to be honest.

ROSE. He's a child.

JIMMY. He's seventeen. And he's borrowing his uncle's transit,
so… I say 'borrow' – I'm not sure his uncle knows much
about it.

ROSE. When did you get so… so old?

JIMMY. Had a spurt, didn't I? (*Beat.*) It'll be alright. It's going
to be good. Fresh start.

ROSE. You don't wish we were staying?

JIMMY. Nah. Not gonna live my whole life here. First man on
Mars, you remember?

ROSE. I do. Don't go too far though.

JIMMY. I am gonna check out who gets our place though.
You're right – never know who they might be.

Move into –

Scene Two

We click forward to 2004. JOY, CONSTANCE, GRACE *and*
GEORGE. *Bags and boxes.*

CONSTANCE. Will we have the same flat when we come back,
or a different one?

JOY. I don't know. We might not –

GEORGE (*to* CONSTANCE). You can pick whatever one you
want.

JOY. Don't –

CONSTANCE (*to* GEORGE). Promise?

JOY. We can't promise that, but we –

CONSTANCE. But we are coming back here?

JOY. Just think of your new house. Think of the red brick and
the bright yellow door and the roses in the garden –

CONSTANCE. For Nana Rose?

JOY. That's right.

CONSTANCE. And strawberries?

JOY. We can try.

CONSTANCE. And my own room?

JOY. Your own room, with your own big bed.

GRACE. I think you'll be spoilt.

CONSTANCE. And a dog.

JOY. I don't know if –

CONSTANCE. You promised. You said the garden was big
enough –

JOY. Let's just get settled in first.

GEORGE (*to* CONSTANCE). Remember, Uncle Eric and I are
just a few streets away.

CONSTANCE. And when do the others get here?

GEORGE. Which others?

JOY. She means the other Liberians. They're arriving soon – very soon.

CONSTANCE (*to* GEORGE). We're a City of Sanctuary – that means somewhere safe.

GRACE. That's right – and it's our job to make them feel welcome.

CONSTANCE. Do you think they'll miss their old home though?

GEORGE. Perhaps. I know I did, at first. But I don't think home is a place, really. I think it's the people you find, and the people you take with you.

CONSTANCE. Do you think my dad's still here? Will he come with us?

JOY. Come on – time to say goodbye.

They exit.

Scene Three

Forward to 2020. POPPY enters, straightens a few things up, pours coffee. NIKKI enters shortly after, just out of the shower. POPPY hands her coffee.

NIKKI. Thanks. I just grabbed a T-shirt from… Think it used to be mine, actually.

POPPY. Keep it.

NIKKI. Do you still sleep in my T-shirts?

POPPY. Don't. I'm not… Letting you sleep on my sofa doesn't change anything. You can drink your coffee and then get on a train, okay?

NIKKI. Okay. (*Beat*.) Only… I don't think there are any trains today.

POPPY. Not my problem.

NIKKI. So… What do adults do on New Year's Day? We could – I know – we could go for a walk in the hills – I hear they have hills here –

POPPY. Don't do this.

NIKKI. Or a pub somewhere. Big old stone pub with proper beer and a real fire, and… and board games. New Year's Day Scrabble tournament –

POPPY. What planet are you on?

NIKKI. I'll let you cheat.

POPPY. Don't.

NIKKI. I'll let you win.

POPPY. I'm not… And I don't cheat! I never cheat!

NIKKI. Uh –

POPPY. I win because I'm better at Scrabble than you, that's it.

NIKKI. Better prove it then.

POPPY. You can't just… (*She stops herself*.) What do you want, Nikki?

NIKKI. I want to talk. (*Beat*.) Cos we never did – not really. You just packed up and left, more or less overnight, so –

POPPY. I had good reason.

NIKKI. Maybe I did too. (*Beat*.) No, not a good reason, there can't be a… But it was hard. It was hard when you couldn't love me like I loved you.

POPPY. I loved you.

NIKKI. I know. But it was different, wasn't it? I love you in technicolour. I love you in five dimensions. I love you in this glorious, messy, destructive… It isn't polite, how I feel about you. It isn't civilised. But that doesn't make it lesser. It was never difficult to love you, but it is difficult to be in love with someone who finds your love embarrassing. And you did. I know you did.

POPPY. That isn't true.

NIKKI. It is. And I get it. Who would want a lifetime of me? Sure, it's fun for a while, but till death do us part? It's a lot. So you started shutting down, shutting me out even more than normal. I was overspilling with all this love and it was too much, because I'm too much, and –

POPPY. Stop it.

NIKKI. I'm just trying to explain.

POPPY. You cheated because you loved me too much?

NIKKI. No.

POPPY. You really will just say anything, won't you?

NIKKI. I'm sorry. I am. Just tell me what else do you need.

POPPY. You really think it's that simple, don't you? Not this – I don't need this. I needed kindness – to be treated with kindness – and patience, and space, and... delicacy. I needed *time* – and you knew that. Not grand gestures. Not declarations. The gesture isn't for me, it's for you. I never asked for this.

NIKKI. I love you. Not a day goes by when I'm not in love with you.

POPPY. I know. But so what, Nikki? I'm not... I can't... I can forgive you – I *have* forgiven you, but I can't deal with all this... I don't want fireworks. I'm not going to chase after you in the rain. And I know you think this is so romantic, this fucking wrecking-ball approach to adult relationships, but it doesn't work for me. You can't keep doing this. You need to go.

NIKKI. Okay. Okay, I've said what I came here to say, so... And I was wrong about this place – wrong about it being

wrong for you. It's nice, and I'm glad you feel settled here.
But you are here by yourself, aren't you?

POPPY. That isn't any of your business.

NIKKI. Don't leave it too long. Not because of what I did.
I couldn't bear that. Find someone who deserves you.
Because until you let someone else in, it's just another box to
keep out the rain. (*Beat*.) Look after yourself, Pops.

NIKKI *goes. Music under.* POPPY *rests her head in her
hands. A moment later* CONNIE *appears behind her. She is
a memory.*

CONNIE. That's you all set then. Happy?

POPPY. It's beautiful, isn't it?

CONNIE. I think so. Bit different from when I grew up round
here –

POPPY. I can imagine.

CONNIE. But that's no bad thing. New lick of paint, new lease
of life. Right time for a new set of people.

POPPY. Yeah.

Music starts.

(*Under her breath*.) Fuck it. Nikki! Nikki!

POPPY *exits, chasing after* NIKKI. *In* 2004 JOY, GRACE,
GEORGE *and* CONSTANCE *enter with bags/boxes, leaving
the flat for the final time.* CONNIE *watches them.*

JOY. All done. Come on, Constance.

CONSTANCE. Goodbye, kitchen. Goodbye, walls. Goodbye,
scary sink. Goodbye, rubbish oven. Goodbye, smelly hall –

JOY. Yes – goodbye, house. (*To* GEORGE.) Can you take
Constance downstairs? I just need to read the meter.

GEORGE (*to* CONSTANCE). Come on, sweetheart.

GRACE *and* GEORGE *go.* CONSTANCE *starts to follow
when she seems to spot* CONNIE *and pauses.* CONNIE
sings to her.

Song: 'Don't Get Hung Up in Your Soul'

CONNIE. WHERE YOU GONNA GO
  NOW THEY'VE CLOSED THE OLD HOME DOWN?
  AND EVERYBODY'S LET YOU DOWN
  BUT YOU'RE THE BEAUTY OF THE TOWN
  BABY, DON'T GET HUNG UP IN YOUR SOUL
  DON'T LET 'EM MAKE YOUR HEART GROW OLD
  DON'T GET HUNG UP IN YOUR SOUL
  BABY, DON'T GET HUNG UP IN YOUR SOUL

  CONSTANCE *goes off.* _1989_. ROSE *and teenage* JIMMY
  cross with their final possessions.

JIMMY. I can take that.

ROSE. I'm not feeble – I can manage. Just let me catch my
  breath.

CONNIE. YOU'RE THE ONE WHO'S SEEN
  THE DARKNESS ON THE EDGE OF TOWN
  YOU'RE THE ONE MY ARM'S AROUND
  YOU'RE THE THORN AND YOU'RE THE CROWN
  BABY, DON'T GET HUNG UP IN YOUR SOUL
  DON'T LET 'EM MAKE YOUR HEART GROW OLD
  DON'T GET HUNG UP IN YOUR SOUL
  BABY, DON'T GET HUNG UP IN YOUR SOUL

ROSE. Right – onwards.

  ROSE *goes.* CONNIE *and* JIMMY *harmonise for a moment.*

JIMMY/CONNIE. DON'T LET 'EM MAKE YOUR HEART
    GROW OLD
  DON'T GET HUNG UP IN YOUR SOUL

  JOY *joins them.*

JIMMY/CONNIE/JOY. BABY, DON'T GET HUNG UP IN
    YOUR SOUL

  JIMMY *goes.*

CONNIE. AND DON'T IT MAKE YOUR HEART
    GROW COLD?

CONNIE *goes. In* 2020, POPPY *catches up with* NIKKI *on the balcony.*

POPPY. Nikki! Wait, just… Jesus, am I doing this? Chasing after you like… Unbelievable.

NIKKI. What?

POPPY. And you knew, didn't you? You knew I'd follow – you were counting on it. You and your Richard Curtis bullshit. Fuck!

NIKKI. Are you okay?

POPPY. You love me, and what does that mean? You'll move up here – start a life with me here, halloumi skewers and all?

NIKKI. Okay.

POPPY. Why? I'm a nightmare. I know I'm not easy. I know historically I haven't… I have got better – since being here I have got better. But this is my home now. And you want this?

NIKKI. If you're here I want it. I want all of it. I want us to buy a cottage and rip up the floorboards and grow old together and both die on the same day and get eaten by our cats. That's all I've ever wanted.

POPPY. Okay.

NIKKI. Okay?

POPPY. Okay.

POPPY *instigates a kiss. Beat.*

Brunch?

NIKKI. Or brunch, sure.

POPPY. I've been invited to a New Year's Day brunch a few floors up. I've baked for it, so I have to drop by.

NIKKI. Right.

POPPY. You could come if you wanted.

NIKKI. Yeah?

POPPY. Yeah. I am better here. I'd like to show you.

NIKKI. New Year, new us?

POPPY. Okay. Then let's make it a good one. I guess make yourself at home.

POPPY *takes* NIKKI*'s hand and they go.*

Scene Four

2004. JOY *is in her empty flat, taking a final look around. She hears the voice of the housing* OFFICER *from her very first day.*

OFFICER (*voice-over*). Here's your kitchen. Sink, for water. Oven here. And the front door – always lock this door. Keep it locked. Always.

JOY *steps out of the flat and into the hallway, locking the door behind her. 1989* JIMMY *is there.*

JOY. Jimmy?

JIMMY. What's that face in aid of?

JOY. You didn't come home.

JIMMY. It's nice to meet you, Joy.

JOY. It was my fault. I kept you here. I shouldn't have.

JIMMY. You live here, do you? You – in here?

JOY. Not any more.

JIMMY. Nice one. Good place, is this.

JOY. Not any more.

JIMMY. I should leave you to it.

JOY. Don't go again.

JIMMY. I could check in on you, if you like? Make sure you're getting no bother.

JOY. Yes. Please.

JIMMY. You don't have to answer – maybe can't answer, but I will. If that's okay? Okay.

JOY. Wait –

JIMMY. Anywhere you are, that's fine by me – that's home.

JOY. Please –

JIMMY. Ta-ra now.

JOY. Ta-ra, duck.

JIMMY *starts to go.* JIMMY *stops. He turns back to her.*

JIMMY. Oh, there was just one other thing.

JOY. Yes? Hello?

JIMMY *smiles. The 'I love you' neon flickers on.* JIMMY *goes.* JOY *stays watching as* CONNIE *appears on the bridge for the final time.* ROSE, NIKKI *and* POPPY *will come to join* JOY *during the speech.*

CONNIE. And so it goes.
    Or so it goes sometimes
    Uncertain souls, pinning too much on a single sunrise,
    Greedily eyeing the horizon
    For a scratch-card *ex machina*
    A thunderbolt sign
    Writ large in neon, if you like
    A reassurance there'll be something left
    Once the shine's worn off
    That their foundations are solid
    That they are stronger than the monolith
    Oh, it's the hope that kills you
    But also keeps you alive
    Without it, this little box could never keep out the rain.
    So they hold their breath
    Because this moment will never come again.

Song: 'As the Dawn Breaks' (Reprise)

ROSE. AS THE DAWN BREAKS
   OVER ROOF SLATES
   HOPE HUNG ON EVERY WASHING LINE

JOY. AS YOUR HEART ACHES
   OVER LIFE'S FATE
   I KNOW WE NEVER HAD MUCH TIME

POPPY/NIKKI. FOR US TO GIVE
   BUT WE DID
   THERE'S SOMETHING IN THOSE DEEP BLUE EYES

The full COMPANY *join them.*

COMPANY. AS THE LIGHT CREEPS OVER THE HOUSES
   AND THE SLATES ARE DARKED BY RAIN
   IN THIS MORNING SEARCH FOR MEANING
   I HEAR A SONGBIRD'S MELODY
   I HEAR A SONGBIRD'S MELODY

ROSE, JOY, POPPY *and* NIKKI *sing the final line, looking out to an uncertain future.*

ROSE/JOY/POPPY/NIKKI. AND SHE'S SINGING JUST
   FOR ME

End.

Acknowledgements

All words and music by Richard Hawley.

'Time Is' (2019)
'My Little Treasures' (2019)
Both copyright © BMG Rights Management (UK).
All rights reserved. Reprinted by permission.

'As the Dawn Breaks' (2009)
'Naked in Pitsmoor' (2001)
'I'm Looking for Someone to Find Me' (2007)
'Tonight the Streets Are Ours' (2007)
'Open Up Your Door' (2009)
'Coles Corner' (2005)
'There's a Storm A-Comin'' (2011)
'Standing at the Sky's Edge' (2012)
'Our Darkness' (2007)
'Midnight Train' (2019)
'For Your Lover Give Some Time' (2009)
'After the Rain' (2009)
'Don't Get Hung Up in Your Soul' (2009)
All copyright © Universal Music Publishing Ltd.
All rights reserved. Reprinted by permission.

A LITTLE NIGHT MUSIC
Stephen Sondheim and Hugh Wheeler

LONDON ROAD
*Alecky Blythe and Adam Cor*k

MISS YOU LIKE HELL
Quiara Alegría Hudes and Erin McKeown

THE NEW AMERICAN MUSICAL
Edited by Wiley Hausam
RENT – *Jonathan Larson*
FLOYD COLLINS – *Tina Landau and Adam Guettel*
THE WILD PARTY – *Michael John LaChiusa and George C. Wolfe*
PARADE – *Alfred Uhry and Jason Robert Brown*

NEXT TO NORMAL
Brian Yorkey and Tom Kitt

ONCE
Enda Walsh, Glen Hansard and Markéta Irglová

PACIFIC OVERTURES
Stephen Sondheim and John Weidman

PASSION
Stephen Sondheim and James Lapine

ROAD SHOW
Stephen Sondheim and John Weidman

THE SECRET GARDEN
Marsha Norman and Lucy Simon

SPRING AWAKENING
Steven Sater and Duncan Sheik

A STRANGE LOOP
Michael R. Jackson

SUNDAY IN THE PARK WITH GEORGE
Stephen Sondheim and James Lapine

SWEENEY TODD
Stephen Sondheim and Hugh Wheeler

URINETOWN
Greg Kotis and Mark Hollmann

www.nickhernbooks.co.uk

facebook.com/nickhernbooks

twitter.com/nickhernbooks